What Did You Do in the War?

What Did You Do in the War?

Peter Morrissey's World War II
Diaries and Letters

written and
edited by

Mickey Morrissey

Typeset in Garamond
Printed and bound by CPI Group (UK) Ltd, Croydon, CR0 4YY

ISBN: 978-1-909075-87-0

Captain P.A. Morrissey
Irish Guards
1943-1947

DEDICATION

This book is dedicated to my brothers,

Charles
Anthony
Paddy

and All Ranks Irish Guards.

CONTENTS

INTRODUCTORY NOTE

The following diary and letter entries were written through the eyes of a 20-year-old platoon commander in the Irish Guards. Little or no thought was given to the wider picture of the strategy or plans behind the last nine months of the Second World War. The priority for my father was to look after his men and get through each day as it came. The entries are for the most part accurate, so spelling (Jeff as opposed to Geoff) or grammatical errors are reported as they were written. Wherever possible I have verified names of people and places, but on the odd occasion this has proved to have been impossible.

FOREWORD

W hat did you do in the war? This is a question that countless boys of my generation asked their fathers. I suspect that if there was an answer it would usually have been, "Nothing very much", and that would have been the end of it.

When my father was posted on active service he kept two diaries, to my knowledge, and wrote nearly 50 letters home to his parents and sisters. What follows is his story from landing in France in September 1944 to V.E. Day, 8th May 1945.

My aim in publishing this book is to preserve this account for his family. However, I also served in the Irish Guards from 1977-1989 and consider the 'Micks' to be my second family. Many of those mentioned in the following pages are familiar names to me and other officers of my generation – in fact, I served with their sons and their grandsons now serve in the Regiment. So this is a short book for all of my father's family, including the Micks.

A very modest gentleman, he hardly ever spoke about his life in the Micks, although once I was commissioned the odd nugget of information would come out!

A couple of points are worth dwelling on before beginning his story. First, it might seem odd to today's generation that he makes so much about going to mass or receiving Holy Communion, but in fact this is not the case. It is quite common in periods of extreme danger for people to recognise God and the comfort that faith can bring.

Whilst on active service, either in the past or today, this remains the case. It was not unusual in the post-war years for ex-serviceman to take up Holy Orders. There is a famous depiction of the Irish Guards in 'Prayer before Battle' described by Kipling as follows:

Shortly before dawn on 15 September 1916, Fr Brown of the 1st Battalion came forward and collected half companies or groups of men as he could find them. Together they knelt on the shell churned ground, Protestant and Catholic, bare headed, their rifles with bayonets fixed by their sides while the small seemingly insignificant figure of the priest gave them Absolution. This simple scene seemed somehow to throw into relief the squalor and the filth, the glory and the sacrifice, which was their war.

This action was to be repeated in Kuwait in 2003 before entering Iraq.

I was privileged to command Number One Company of the 1st Battalion Irish Guards and know only too well the importance of the relationship between the Company Commander and his officers and senior non-commissioned officers. Today the first Christmas card of the year I receive, and send, is to the widow of my Company Sergeant Major, Paddy Lavery. You will see, as my father's story unfolds, how his relationship with his Company Commander, Edward Fisher-Rowe, develops over the months they serve together.

During the Second World War the Irish Guards lost in all 734 dead, including 59 officers, of which 17 died during the nine months that are reported on in this book. The names of these officers can be found at the back.

Finally, I have included as an appendix, the story of Lieutenant Michael Cambier, which took over 50 years to come to light. Michael was the only child of Colonel Val Cambier who was my grandmother's first cousin. Also an Old Amplefordonian, he was commissioned into the Parachute Regiment and dropped into Arnhem for Operation Market Garden. His tragic story resulted in a close relationship between my father and Colonel Val, who after the war became one of my brother's godfathers, I suspect there is no one left today to remember Michael Cambier.

Quis Seperabit

Captain P.H. Morrissey M.B.E.
Royal Navy
1910-1948

CHAPTER 1
JOINING UP

Born on 7th June 1924 in Plymouth to Commander and Mrs Bernadette (Baba) Morrissey my Father, Peter Anthony Filose Morrissey, came from a family that had served kings, queens, maharajahs and country for 250 years. His maternal grandfather, Colonel Sir Clement Filose, served in the Indian Army in the early part of the twentieth century, whilst his uncle Brigadier Tony Filose served in King George V's Own Central India Horse in North Africa during the Second World War. Meanwhile his father, Captain Patrick Henry Morrissey MBE, served in the Royal Navy during both World Wars.

It was therefore unsurprising that whilst at Ampleforth College he was a successful member of the O.T.C. [Officer Training Corps], being promoted to the rank of sergeant prior to leaving the school. His housemaster, Father Wright OSB, wrote in his 1940 Autumn Term report, "He did particularly well to obtain his Certificate 'A' in the O.T.C. and I hope that if this leads to jobs requiring leadership and command he will take every opportunity that comes his way."

Father Dolly Brooks, a friend of my grandmother, served in two World Wars and in peace with the Irish Guards, first as a subaltern under his great friend Alex, the future Field Marshal Lord Alexander of Tunis, and second as a chaplain in North Africa and at Anzio, where he won the Military Cross for extreme gallantry and devotion to duty. He is probably the only chaplain who took half-a-dozen prisoners

Regimental Headquarters,

Irish Guards,

Birdcage Walk,

London, S.W. 1.

21st September, 1942.

Dear

     As you were told when you were last here, we shall definitely be able to accept you as a candidate for a commission in the Irish Guards.

     Will you please report here in the afternoon of the 1st October and we will give you directions as to where and when you should report on the 2nd October.

     I think I have given you all the information about what to bring, and if there is anything else you will want to know, will you write and ask me as soon as possible.

     For your information here are the dates and places where you should go for your training:

Depot:-	2nd October - 4th December.	
Training Bn. Scots Guards:-	4th December - 25th January, '43	
Wrotham Selection Depot:-	25th January - 5th February, '43	
161st O.C.T.U., Aldershot:-	5th February - 4th June.	

Yours

[signature]

Lieutenant,
A/Regimental Adjutant, Irish Guards.

P.A. Morrissey, Esq.,
24 Radiden,
Manor Road,
Hove.

armed only with his breviary and a blackthorn stick. There is no doubt that Father Dolly's advice and influence helped my father decide that he should enlist into the Irish Guards, commonly known as 'The Micks'.

His application to join the regiment was submitted and references were taken from Ampleforth as to whether or not he would make suitable officer material.

On 23rd September 1942 his housemaster wrote to his mother as follows:

> *Dear Mrs Morrissey,*
> *Very many thanks for your letters.*
> *I have already replied to the request from the Irish Guards to give my opinion of Peter, when they arrived. I had also heard from Father Rudesind [Dolly Brooks]. Rest assured that I couldn't give anything but a good report about Peter. I am sure he will do very well and I wish him all the best of luck....*
> *It must be bad enough for you having a husband serving – and now a son. Bare up and be brave and trust in God's goodness.*
> *Yours very sincerely,*
> *Maurice Wright.*

On the same day, 23rd September, as the above letter arrived so too did a letter from the headmaster of Ampleforth (overleaf).

Having completed the necessary documentation Peter Morrissey was enlisted into the 'NORMAL REGULAR ARMY' Irish Guards on 2nd October 1942 and promptly dispatched to attend Sgt P Schofield's Brigade Squad at the Guards' Depot in November 1942.

TELEGRAMS:
  AMPLEFORTH-COLLEGE

STATION:
  GILLING, L.N.E.R.

TELEPHONE:
  AMPLEFORTH 224.

AMPLEFORTH COLLEGE,
YORK.

23 September 1942

Dear Mrs Morrissey,

I am very glad to hear that Peter has been accepted for the Irish Guards and I wish him the very best of luck. He will find some other Amplefordians in the regiment, and I think that he should be very happy there.

I enclose the certificate you sent me to sign. I understand you have written to Fr Terence independently.

With kind regards,

Yours sincerely,

Letter from the headmaster of Ampleforth

Sgt. P. Schofield's   Brigade Squad.

GUARDS DEPOT   NOVEMBER, 1942.

G. & B. BUNCE

PHOTOGRAPHERS

Gdsn. J. R. Mitchell, R. Hanzay, G. D. Roberts, P. M. Forrester, D. R. G. Noel, Sgt. W. Glynn, Gdsn. K. Mahaffy, D. A. Rogers, T. A. Jones, R. D. H. Crewdson, A. Seaward, D. S. D. Galloway
(P.T. Instr.)   Gdsn. A. Seaward, T.U.S. D. Reynolds
T.U.S. S. Langford, Gdsn. The Lord Plunket,   H. C. H. Bowser, E. W. Traford, D. G. Humphreys, M. O. Stanley, H. Whitwell
  Gdsn. K. N. Manners, G. H. Legge, J. V. B. De Saumarez, A. D. Trenchard Cox, F. A. Mortimer, H. C. H. Bowser, Col. W. H. Webb, Sgt. T. Ferguson, Gdsn. M. N. Gilbey, M. F. V. Baillie
Gdsn. H. H. Spencer, Lord Balgonis   Sgt. D. Bartlett, C.S.M. T. Jones, SGT. P. SCHOFIELD, Major H. T. Rice,   Gdsn. J. D. Siddeley, A. D. G. Langmead
Gdsn. J. A. Maxtone-Graham,   (W.T. Instr.)   (Asst. Squad Instr.) (Squad Instr.)   (W.T. Instr.)

7

The aim of Brigade Squad was to give recruits, who were deemed to be potential officers and taken from some of the leading public schools in the country, the experience of what guardsman went through in their basic training prior to passing out and being posted to their regiments. Brigade Squad was a tough physical course usually lasting eight weeks in all and designed to stretch those that attended to their utmost limits. It was intentionally significantly harder than infantry basic training and was respected by all ranks as such. It was a learning curve that ensured that those potential officers who eventually received a commission (and the success rate was low) would understand what guardsman had been through in training. Similarly, guardsman and non-commissioned officers had respect for officers who turned up in positions of command some months or years later. I attended my Brigade Squad in 1977 and subsequently went on to command three Brigade Squads in the early 1980s.

From the Guards Depot to the 161st O.C.T.U. [Officer Cadet Training Unit] at Aldershot for officer training and finally a commission in the Irish Guards, 2nd Lieutenant Peter Morrissey was posted to the Training Battalion Irish Guards, based at Hobbs Barracks Lingfield, on 4th June 1943.

Little is known of the intervening period other than he was admitted to Botley Park Hospital on 9th November 1943 to have a cartilage operation, thereby preventing him from joining the 1st Battalion in the disastrous Anzio campaign which took place in January 1944. Had this not happened, as he regularly pointed out, he would not have been alive to have witnessed the end of the war.

Convalescence appears to have been spent with the remnants of the 1st Battalion in Scotland during 1944, including attending Course No 19 (Platoon Commanders Wing) School of Infantry at Barnard Castle in April and May that year, together with an attachment to the Westminster Garrison Battalion in London.

On 18th August 1944 he received a telegram ordering him to report for duty on 28th August in readiness to join the 3rd Battalion Irish Guards in North West Europe.

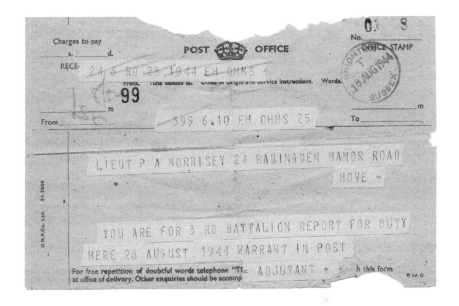

LIEUT P A MORRISEY 24 RADINGDEN MANOR ROAD HOVE =

YOU ARE FOR 3 RD BATTALION REPORT FOR DUTY HERE 28 AUGUST 1944 WARRANT IN POST ADJUTANT

CHAPTER 2
SEPTEMBER '44

Operation Market Garden took place in September 1944. Cornelius Ryan, the author of *A Bridge Too Far*, wrote:

> *The date was September 17th, 1944, the 263rd week of World War II. Very few among the onlookers knew they were witnessing the first phase of Operation Market-Garden – Field Marshall Montgomery's daring and brilliant plan to end the war within a few weeks.*

At the final conference at Montgomery's headquarters a week before, Lieutenant General Frederick (Boy) Browning, Deputy Commander of the First Allied Airborne Army, had asked how long it would take to reach the airborne troops. Montgomery replied, "Two days." Browning looked at the map and said, "But, sir, I think we might be going a bridge too far." Arnhem was 64 miles behind the German lines.

This miscalculation on Montgomery's part was to prove expensive. Over 17,000 Allied soldiers – British, American and Polish – were killed, wounded or missing, considerably more than in the D-Day landings.

The Irish Guards Group consisting of the 2nd and 3rd Battalions Irish Guards were to lead the Guards Armoured Division and XXX Corps into Holland. The Commanding Officer of the 3rd Battalion, Lieutenant Colonel J.O.E. Vandeleur (who was played by Michael Caine in the film *A*

Bridge Too Far) was tasked to lead the attack up the single track road. Many years later I had the honour of commanding the bearer party at Brigadier Joe's funeral at Brookwood Cemetery, Pirbright.

The first of over 40 letters sent from my father whilst on active service is opposite and describes his last few hours in England before departing for the front line.

To: Mrs P.H. Morrissey
45 Salisbury Road, Southsea Hants

3rd Bn Irish Guards
B.L.F. [British Liberation Force]
3rd Sept [1944]

My Darlings,

How are you all? If I tell you I'm in the pink do you know what I mean? I think it means I'm feeling grand anyway that's just about it. Actually I started a letter to you on the train from Edinburgh but the damn thing rocked about so much that I just couldn't control the pencil and as you would not be able to read it I tore it up. But now in this short respite I will recommence and, I hope, finish and send it.

Thank you for your very nice letters two of which you sent before you got mine but no doubt you will have written again. They informed me on Wednesday and Jeff Warnock from the 1st and myself took trains to Kings X. On arriving there I went to the hotel, had a good breakfast and a bath!!! Then I dumped my kit half at Norrie's and half at Waterloo. Then Norrie gave me a drink at Manettas. After which I rushed along to the Ritz to meet Jeff. He turned up and we had a grand luncheon at the Berkeley with a bottle of Champagne-Cider the accent being on the cider. I rang up Lynette to tell her that her case was at 38 and although she was going to the theatre she insisted on coming over to the Berkeley and indeed wanted to see us off at 3.20. However I managed to dissuade her as it seemed quite pointless and anyway I hate being seen off really.

There's such a lot I'd like to tell you but all I can say is that the way things are going at present I shouldn't be at all surprised if it's all over by the 1st October which I believe was the original date given by the Yanks some time ago.

Did I tell you about the party I had with Barbara on Thursday night. I took her to De Surgs and we had a grand time dancing and dining. The next day I had lunch with them all at the flat and Barbara presented me with a wonderful lighter and a very charming photograph of herself. The lighter is simply wizard it will work in any wind and I was awfully pleased to get it. I heard today that Andrew Nielson was killed by his wounds. Rupert Mahaffy and Dennis Galloway are out already in the 3rd. I saw Brian the other day and he seems furious at being left behind.

Well, I must close now and get a wash I am going to send home some sheets I think, if I can get them parcelled up and can send them. I must also get a wash as I feel filthy already. So long and keep well and don't worry about me, I'll keep behind some big guardsmen alright.

Tons + Tons of love from your loving son

    Peter

P.S Give my love to Patricia & Cherub and tell them I'll be writing soon.

Monday 4th September
Left Aldershot 3 a.m. March to Station – arrives in marshalling area near S'hampton. Confined to Camp. Saw "Hit Parade of 1943" in a tent. – Rain positively awful.

Tuesday 5th September – 1910hrs
Left Southampton, New Docks to American destroyer. Lovely blue sky. Lay off Portsmouth all night.

Wednesday 6th September
Sailed 0650 hrs fairly choppy to start, calmed this side though, amazing number of ships crossing arrived Arromanches beaches. Marched to 60 Hamit Camp. Just by P.O.W. [Prisoner of War] Camp, Thousands & Thousands (6,700) a goodly sight!
Took a walk round P.O.W. Camp dreadful, looking types, mostly mongul. Bedded down in tent. It started to rain.

Thursday 7th September
Rained all night – one P.O.W. died during the night through exposure. I slept well, cooked some porridge, rather good. Packed up and left. – in mud and rain – at 3 p.m. arrived at 46 R.H.U. [Reinforcement Holding Unit] at 6 p.m. (Bayeux) looks very comfortable.

Friday 8th September
Parade in Coy [Company] lines – went to Bayeux, saw Cathedral & replica of tapestry – drank some Calvados – Inhabitants seem hostile – came back to bed.

Saturday 9th September
Lovely day – wrote to Babara then took a ride out to Caen with Bill, saw the battle fields – masses of burnt out tanks – went round Cathedral not as nice as Bayeux Cathedral. Has been hit. Talked French with some mechanics – Drove back. And so to bed.

To: Mrs P.H. Morrissey
       45 Salisbury Road, Southsea Hants

3rd Bn Irish Guards

B.L.A

9th Sept [1944]

My Darling Baba and Pat,

Here we are again! Only as you can see by the address further up the line. We arrived yesterday after the foulest journey I've ever done. Of course I saw quite a bit of the countryside, but other than that there isn't anything to say for it. We are in a lovely old chateau which was occupied by the Gestapo as a headquarters. And at the back in the woods there are some very deep pits where they used to throw French men down. The bodies have only just been removed and the place just aint healthy what absolute swine they are though. They wrecked this place before leaving and booby-trapped it. But I don't think anyone has got hurt that way. The people from the village were up here looking round. All in black and crying their eyes out it was pathetic to watch. They're all far more pleasant around here which is a great help I suppose it's only natural though after what the Hun did. How are the Buzz Bombs? I hope they're not sending too many our way. I got one of your letters the other day but nothing else yet. However they'll turn up sometime I expect. I'm sorry this is short but I will write again as soon as possible. Meanwhile take care of yourselves my darlings and lets pray this war will be over in double-quick time. All the best and tons and tons of love from Peter xxxxxx

To: Mrs P.H. Morrissey
        45 Salisbury Road, Southsea Hants

40 R.H.U

B.L.A

10th Sept 1944

My darling Baba and Pat,

... Bill and I went to a town about 10 miles from here yesterday and went round a Cathedral rather good but not so nice as the first one we saw. Then we had a grand time with two Frenchmen carrying on in French only. It was rather fun. After we had been speaking quite a bit one of them motioned me and showed me a Jerry steel helmet he had hung up in his garage. He was very proud of it. We asked him what became of the Hun and he replied. "Il est mort"!!

Drink is very hard to get here and impossible by the bottle but further in at some other places it may be quite easy. And, of course, everything is a shocking price, perhaps, you can imagine. No food is allowed to be bought and as I say things are generally pretty stiff but I think it should be better up the line.

Well, Baba, give my love to all at home and send me an occasional line some time, meanwhile I'll keep writing and don't worry about me – promise?

Goodbye for the present

        With tons and tons of love

                From Peter

xxxxxx

Sunday 10th September
Lovely Day again – rotten cold sprung up during night orderly officer today – very dull.

Monday 11th September
Still got bloody cold – have to guard officer, who deserted for 24 hrs starting 6 P.M.

Tuesday 12th September
Still got cold – guarded prisoner all today.
Saw film, small French children smoking, very funny.

Wednesday 13th September
Cold still with me – went into Bayeux, had long conversation with French woman, felt like death in the afternoon so went to bed. Life very dull.

Thursday 14th September
Rained during night but sun has come out now.
Cold nearly gone.
Hear we are off Saturday not certain yet.

Friday 15th September
Lecture on air photography, quite good.
Going tomorrow definite to Amiens to join 40 R.H.U.
Conversation with pessimistic Dutch Colonel. Too bad!
Had three whiskies – grand!
But bed summons me!
(Received first letter from Baba Ce Soir!!)

Saturday 16th September
Arose 0630 Breakfast 0700hrs, Left Camp 46 0815hrs marched to Bayeux entrained for Amiens. Sold 40 cigs for 50 francs, travelled in train through Caen had a meal and moved across in transport to Rouen, very cold and dark. Departed Rouen 0530 by train and arrived in Amiens 1630 there.

Sunday 17th September

After sleeping all night in a freezing carriage the train departed from Rouen at 0530 hrs. The journey was very long and tiring and we arrived at Amiens at 1630 hrs. Here three of us split a bottle of champagne, 300 frs. Travelled to a Chateau (40 R.H.U). This had been Gestapo headquarters. I saw a pit where hostages were thrown in after being killed. It stank to heaven. Relatives of the hostages were there taking a look around. All very pathetic. Went to bed and kept gun at the ready.

Monday 18th September

Explored Chateau and then packed up to move on. Got in transport 1600hrs. Drove to station 20 miles and waited till 2200hrs in a field.

Boarded a train bound for Brussels. Put up Camp bed in truck and went to sleep, train departed 2400hrs.

Tuesday 19th September

Awoke at 0730hrs at Arras. Arose at 1000hrs packed up kit and watched the countryside go by.

People very pleased to see us gave us fruit of all kinds apples – pears – peaches etc. Stopped at Tournai for lunch just inside border of Belgium.

Arrived at Enghien nine o'clock. Had to march five and a half miles to camp.

Had very excellent dinner and masses of Brandy felt very merry. Retired to bed.

Wednesday 20th September

Arose a neuf heures. Had breakfast and did damn-all else all day. We are in a farm house and it is very pleasant indeed, we sleep in tents in an orchard. But we are off to the front line within an hour's notice. The Drink is very excellent here.

No transport has arrived so am off to bed. Expect to move out at 0530hrs.

To: Pay Capt. P.H. Morrissey M.B.E. R.N.
        45 Salisbury Road, Southsea Hants

B.L.A
20th Sept [1944]

My dearest Pat,

A very Happy Birthday to you and may you have many more. A trifle late I'm sorry to say but all the same I remembered it. Tell me all about it and how you spent it no doubt in the office. I wish I could get a bottle of this Cognac brandy over to you, its smashing stuff.

Did I tell you that on arriving at Amiens myself and another officer split a bottle of Champagne and the funny part about it all was it merely made me incredibly sleepy but not in the least bit elated. However it is not too easy to come by as I thought it would be at first. One bottle cost 300 frs which is 30/s and quite expensive as drinks go out here. Still if I knew I was coming home tomorrow I'd certainly bring some back. Please excuse the pencil I hate writing with it but it's all I've got I'm afraid. The Belgians seem very pleased to see us all here and give us masses of fruit which is a good thing. How are things going as regards the house and have you left 45 Salisbury Road yet I send all the letters there as they will turn up sooner or later I hope.

I'm sorry this is short but there is not a lot one can say at present. I wrote to Patricia recently so she'll have what news there is.

Goodbye then and god bless you have a good birthday and will be there for your next.

From Peter

Thursday 21st September

Awoke but still no sign of any transport.

Will move off as soon as it arrives.

Nothing much doing till 1230 when transport arrived. Had lunch and got packed aboard. Departed 1400hrs.

Went through Brussells, lovely city, everyone throwing kisses & cheering. Crossed Albert Canal and was given peaches & pears, more cheering!

Arrived Hechtel x Roads (Div H.Q) [Divisional Headquarters] 1930hrs. Had dinner, went to bed in mess tent. Opened 6 bottles of Champagne. The astonishing thing is that we never seem to be expected by anyone and on arrival they always seem to be departing in the near future.

Friday 22nd September

Expected to move on up the line any moment. Everything packed up and ready to move. It's always the same!!

This place is like the training area of Aldershot and was in fact training area for Belgian Army in peace time – masses of supplies passing up to front line. It's raining at present.

Heard the road further up has been cut by the Hun. Thus the G.A.D. [Guards Armoured Division] is cut off. Our move has been delayed.

Had dinner & drank some wine.

Went to bed.

Saturday 23rd September

It rained all night however "slept like a log" arose 0800 had breakfast and heard the Hun has been pushed back off the road by 1100 rumours we are moving up at 1600 hrs today still raining life pretty dull.

Half an hour's notice to move off all packed up – started in convoy 1600hrs at 2000hrs my driver ditched one wheel – got the truck out and ditched it again this time it was impossible to get the truck out so the men lay down either side of the road and went to sleep. Two people stayed up all night – masses of transport going up the road – The village ahead was being shelled & mortared all night. Hence the convoys had to stop. Plenty of noise

Sunday 24th September
At 0700hrs Sgt. Rennold and I walked 3½ miles to Eindhoven and collected a break-down gang. These soon got us out of the ditch and again, we set off. But all on our own. Passed the road that the Hun had cut (quite a lot of smashed vehicles and dead men, poor fellows). Luckily no shells came our way. Just passed Uden when my driver crashed into a carrier and smashed the left hand spring completely. Thus matters couldn't have been worse. However the 1st Grens [1st Battalion Grenadier Guards], who had been sent back to deal with the truck, helped us out here and lent us two half-trucks to proceed with. So leaving the driver with the 3 tonner, we came as fast as we could to join the 3rd Battalion. The Bn [Battalion] is out of the front at present and in some houses (very comfortable) was very tired indeed so went to bed after dinner am in No.1 Coy Edward Fisher-Rowe with the 3rd Battalion.

* * *

On the evening of Sunday 24th September seventy men reinforced the Irish Guards Group together with four officers; Lieutenants Billy Reynolds, Dennis Galloway, Geoffrey Warnock and Peter Morrissey.

To: Mrs P.H. Morrissey
        45 Salisbury Road, Southsea Hants

No1 Coy
3rd Battalion Irish Guards
B.L.A
25th Sept [1944]

Baba, Darling and Pat

How are you back there? I am expecting a great pile of mail some say, but twice, as you know, the line was cut no mail has reached us. However the Hun is well out of that now. I hope my letters have been turning up alright. I haven't had the chance of writing for the last few days but I shall write whenever possible. Only please don't worry about me as I am having a wonderful time at present and wouldn't be stuck back in a Tr Bn [Training Battalion] for anything in the world. It may be quite hot at times but it's all in a day's work. The weather here is very changeable. As it started today with a beautiful blue sky and then poured with rain and then the sun came out and now it's raining again. All very trying but still it could be raining all the time. The officers in the Bn are all extremely nice and I think the Commanding Officer is first class. Did you know the Brigade of Guards have made such a name for themselves since they started but they are known by the Hun as "Churchill's Butchers" rather good don't you think? I have been in an orchard, the like of which, I've never seen before (what bad grammar!) but honestly it's <u>huge</u> and has almost every type of fruit lovely pears and Victoria Plums. And there is a massive vineyard at the back with bunches and bunches of blue grapes. On the way up we had from time to time, peaches and pears showered at us. So you can see the life is certainly rewarded with the fruits of other people's labours.

And now tell me, Baba, how is everything going at home ? How is Delia ? And how are the two girls in the services? Tell me what news of the V2 has it done a lot of damage I do so hope not.

Well I'll write again as soon as I can but I must close now. Give my love to Kitty and Daisy when you see them again. Goodbye and God bless you both with all my love from Peter xxxxx

* * *

Monday 25th September   With the 3rd Battalion
Enjoyed a most comfortable sleep and awoke to find a bright blue sky, was introduced to my pl. No3 pl. [Number 3 Platoon] which has a great name for itself (Joe's bridge). Hope to God I can keep that name up for them. Had breakfast and walked around a bit. We are in a huge orchard with every kind of fruit – some Jerry planes came over about 1030 and one came over us at tree level. It's very hard to distinguish between our fire and the Huns no doubt I shall soon be able to. (Have met most of the officers by now and find them all extremely pleasant). A big plane battle took place saw three shot down, one in flames poor fellows, some bailed out. Did nothing much had dinner and went to bed. Quite a bit of gunnery all day.

Tuesday 26th September
Arose and had breakfast bit of a scare about us going out which turned into being at one hour's notice to deal with pockets of resistance further North. Saw a Spitfire shot down. Had a very good dinner party in the Coy mess and retired to bed.

Wednesday 27th September
We are now on 4 hours notice so we went into Nijmegen and had some very good showers, nice and hot. In afternoon inspected the weapons and generally stoodged around. Heard we are moving to Elst tomorrow. Its pouring with rain and altogether the weather is 'not so hot'. We had a big dinner party at which I got rather merry, not a good thing the next morning.

Thursday 28th September

We are moving up to take over in the line in the morning. I held a drill parade after lunch the Pl Comds [Platoon Commanders] and Coy Commander drove up to look at the positions. I am taking over from Robert Gremstone we got shelled whilst I was up. Returned to bring men up. Left 6.30 arrived in dark and took over odd shelling and am I windy?! At 12 p.m. I took a patrol out but had to return owing to the light and flat countryside. But at 1a.m. we went out again, were shelled. Saw and heard nothing. Returned to bed.

Friday 29th September

Awoke at 0530 had some German Coffee & slice of bread, went to Bn HQ [Battalion Headquarters] and reported result of patrol.

Looked round positions and then the shells came. Kept down under and in a little while the F.O.O. [Forward Operation Officer] Arty got his guns onto them. That soon stopped them. He either knocked them out or they withdrew. What's the difference so long as they keep off us. Very quiet afternoon. Thank God. Later our guns put up a terrible barrage on the enemy. Have to take another patrol out tonight. Start at 2200hrs found binoculars by night a great help. Saw nothing. Heard nothing. No enemy actions in sight which is a damned pity.

Saturday 30th September

Had a good sleep though Battle-dress was soaking. Enemy hasn't been shelling since yesterday morning. We are being pulled out tonight to be reserve Company. Had a fine lunch killed and cooked by platoon (1 sheep) Cherries to follow (bottled). Then tea. <u>Smashing</u>. Sun out in afternoon and everything peaceful. What a pity there has to be a war on. The men in my platoon are a very happy lot and morale is certainly very high wish I was back with the family. We moved out after a little shelling back to 2 Coy area. They took over. Settled in quite good. Had dinner and went to bed.

CHAPTER 3
OCTOBER '44

Following the calamitous events of Operation Market Garden the next few weeks saw a period of consolidation. According to the Regimental history both Irish Guards Battalions remained in billets, the 2nd Battalion near Alverna, the 3rd Battalion at Hoogbrek, "a dull flat place, and very wet." They both need the rest to refit and train their new men.

* * *

Sunday 1st October
Awoke to find Edward in a boiling rage as the pl [platoon] was fast asleep and not standing-to all my fault and I feel very bad about it all. At about 6.45 the Hun started shelling. This is awful and nothing can be done but sit still – some pretty close ones – have vowed to visit Lourdes 1 in 2 yrs if the whole pl is brought out of the war alive. I am confident Our Blessed Lady will bring us through all right.
Germans put in infantry attack but were repulsed. We are being shelled on and off all day.

Monday 2nd October
During the night the Hun attacked our forward Coys with Infantry and Tanks. In the morning he overran No2 Coy and William H-Kelly [Harvey-Kelly] knocked out a Panther with a Piat (good for him). Dreadful shelling and mortaring going on but we knocked out 4 tanks altogether on the afternoon we got our Arty [Artillery] and Mortars on to Jerry and pasted him all

over. The Typhoons came in and gave it to him. We move out of the line tonight. Dennis was wounded today. Got a big bunch of mail.

Thursday 3rd October
We moved out last night T.G. [Thank God] quite successfully crossed the Rhine on Bailey Bridge. River lit up by search-lights we are in a farmhouse very nice and how comfortable after the last few days. Its rainy cold today though.
Had a kit inspection and just rested all day – marvellous. Got another lot of mail wrote letters myself.

To: Mrs P.H. Morrissey
       11 Wilberforce Road, Southsea Hants

No1 Coy
3rd Battalion Irish Guards
B.L.A
3rd October [1944]

My darling Baba,

At long last I have received some very, very welcome mail. In fact about 12 letters altogether two from you dated 26th and 28th September. Thank you so much for them both it certainly makes me feel 100% better when the mail turns up.

... The last 4 days have been absolute Hell but thank God I and my platoon are all alright. I wrote a letter to you in the trench which I have sent I hope you got it. It was really a note on a tiny piece of paper, all that I had that that time.

I always thought you read the newspapers inside-out but I see now you can't do, or else you would have seen that the spear-head of the British 2nd army right the way from Bayeaux to Nijmegen has been this Brigade. They've done absolutely wonders and I think it's a great pity that they don't get the publicity they deserve. However after the war maybe someone will give us a write-up. "Thank heavens we have a Brigade of Guards" was a remark passed by one of the Paratroopers.

I am looking forward to the books when they turn up. I hope Cherub had some luck with my Rosary as I should so like to have it again; It was such a lovely one.

God bless you tons and tons of love from your loving son Peter.

To: Pay Capt P.H. Morrissey M.B.E. RN
        11 Wilberforce Road, Southsea Hants

No1 Coy

3rd Battalion Irish Guards

B.L.A

3rd October [1944]

My dearest Pat,

… I do wish the Germans would give in the trouble is they don't know when they are beaten. If only they would pack in then life would be just grand.

It's got very cold here today although yesterday the sun was out and it was lovely and hot. I'm afraid winter has set in and winter in these conditions it's not very pleasant. However we have just got to lump it.

Do you remember my telling you about Dennis Galloway who was an architect? – well he has been wounded though not badly I don't think. He joined the Bn with me. I have been very lucky I think it's all your prayers so thank you very much. I have just received another letter from Patricia the fourth from her so far so I must send her a line. I have written to Baba and I will write again soon to both of you. But just now I have so many to answer so please forgive the abrupt ending and thank you very much for the letters. God bless you and keep you well

Tons and Tons of love from Peter

Wednesday 4th October
A lovely day today had a very good nights rest. Had a parade this morning and got the most frightful rocket from Edward. Am still very thick because of the last time. When will the war be over? Went into N. [Nijmegen] to officers club quite a good place but very crowded. Had a lovely bath came back wrote more letters and went to bed.

Thursday 5th October
Pretty much the same as yesterday went and saw a flick – Bob Hope and D. Lamour.
More welcome letters received

Friday 6th October
Add re-equipment of pl going on.
Otherwise nothing very much this rest is good as the weather is splendid.

Saturday 7th October
Drill parade P.T. [Physical Training] weapon inspection.
Good weather nothing much else.

To: Mrs P.H. Morrissey
        11 Wilberforce Road, Southsea Hants

No1 Coy
3rd Battalion Irish Guards
B.L.A
7th October [1944]

My darlings,

Once again I am writing to you to tell you I'm still OK and "lapping it up "as the guardsmen would say. Which, when translated means resting! No more letters yet but they will still be coming I'm sure. If only we didn't have to censor letters I'd be able to write a lot more. No sooner do I finish a pile than another lot is brought in. However it's a good thing as the men have a great chance to write to everyone and that keeps up the morale. I haven't done a lot since writing last but I went and saw Bob Hope in "They Got Me Covered" with D Lamour, a very good film which I had already seen but thoroughly enjoyed all the same.

Life is not too bad these days but, as you know, the war can't end too soon. I managed to get to mass, confession and communion this morning for which I was very grateful to the Lord. It was a lovely big Franciscan monastery rather modern I should say but it all felt as though it might have been somewhere in England and not somewhere in Holland.

I think I told you about the people I'm billeted with. They are absolutely charming and the Old dame gives me buckets of fresh milk (she must think I look anaemic). It would be so nice to come back after the war and see them that I think I might.

I've got quite a good souvenir off a Jerry prisoner we took, a compass, which I think I'll hang on to. I wish one could buy stuff here but we never go near any shops and we never went near Paris. Still maybe when the war is over I'll take a trip round some of those countries where scent etc. is easily bought and bring some home.

No more for just now but keep smiling and send me a line I'm longing to hear from you all again.

Cheerio and I'll write again soon

Goodbye and God bless you

tons and tons of love from Peter xxxxxxx

* * *

Sunday 8th October
Bit of a scare on about some Paratroops being dropped in the neighbourhood up all night standing-to. More letters and splendid weather.

Monday 9th October
Usual drill Routine Parades. Mens baths Div. [Division] club entertainment. Good weather. Rumours A/P [Anti-Personnel] bombs being dropped. Slit trenches have to be dug.

Tuesday 10th October
Rained all day first bad day for sometime. Stopped in all day, received some mail and wrote letters.

To: Mrs P.H. Morrissey
       11 Wilberforce Road, Southsea Hants

No1 Coy
3rd Battalion Irish Guards
B.L.A
10th October [1944]

Baba dearest,

Once again I am most fortunate in being able to write your letter. We don't really know our movements from day to day. But as you can guess I am still resting and it's very welcome indeed.

... Last night Catholic officers of whom there aren't really many had a cocktail party with the new priest Fr. Hartington. He is from Limerick the same parish as De Valera. He told some amusing tales and one of him being taken prisoner buy some Jerries whom he said were terribly jittery and whom he bluffed into thinking they were surrounded. They held him 3 hours and then they let him go. They didn't even keep his driver as Fr. H said he couldn't drive the jeep himself. And they didn't search the car or else they'd have found a rifle and three Luger Automatics!! Anyway by this bluff he managed to persuade them to let him go. His only regret was that he didn't ask them to surrender to himself and his driver as they might easily have done so, they were in such a bad state.

And, Baba, he told me Fr. Curran had died! R.I.P. He died of heart failure the first night the Armoured Bn were in Brighton. I was sorry to hear that. Did you know?

Well, I must close now but I'll be writing again soon. keep writing to me everyone.

Cheerio and God bless you all

Tons and tons of love from

Peter

Wednesday 11th October
Usual Parades weather cleared up again. Am going to
Brussels tomorrow. No3 Coy had to send out 1 pl to clean up
some Germans but didn't find any.
This rest is damned good.

Thursday 12th October
Barney gave me 2000 frs to get some wine in B. Dick and I
set off in a 15cwt [Morris 15cwt lorry]. Arrived in B in 4 ½
hours. Town major was bloody and wouldn't give us a food
chit or a room to stay in. The N.C.O.s [Non-Commissioned
Officers] were all fine as they had people to go to. Finally a
civilian put us up in their home not too good but better than
nowhere.
Intend to find a room in a hotel tomorrow.

Friday 13th October
Had a <u>small</u> breakfast then took a tram into the city. Got a
room in hotel Amsterdam. Spent morning shopping Some
English Cowboy flick. Then went out to Night Clubs. Very
good cabaret show, much drinking, met a nice girl, Marie,
ate nothing but grapes, meringues and ice-cream.

Saturday 14th October
Started back 2.30 got lost took 6½ hours to get back. Am still
wondering if it was worth it. But hope to go again soon.

Sunday 15th October
Nothing much all day

Monday 16th October
Same but it rained all day

To: Mrs P.H. Morrissey
        11 Wilberforce Road, Southsea Hants

No1 Coy
3rd Battalion Irish Guards
B.L.A
Monday 16th October [1944]

My darling Baba,

… Barney Du Boulay has joined the company as second in Command and little Robin O'Kelly and John Parker have come out (last night) to the company so I am feeling a bit better. I didn't like being the only Platoon Commander with Edward as he is very difficult at times also I like an officer of my own age as you can realise.

… And now you'd like to hear about my 48 hours in that "city of vice", Brussells? Dick Nelson-Bobbett an old Beaumont boy and myself went in on Thursday and got in in 4½ hours (about 160 miles) Good going considering the car was a 15cwt. But the roads for the most part are wonderful. We nearly got kicked out when they heard we were in on leave but as the Commanding Officer has sent us we were damned if we were going all the way back. However we couldn't get in a room anywhere or get any food to eat. So we tried to find a hotel. Whilst asking the way a civilian suggested we spent the night in their house so off we went to the suburb of Brussells where we were given supper and a room. Poor old Dick couldn't speak a word of French but said everything in Spanish or English however they seemed to understand him all right. I managed to make my three words go a long way. In the morning we went into the city to the Gare du Nord. And here we found a small second-rate hotel (no hot water) for 110 francs une nuit. We settled in and then I did some shopping.

After dinner of grapes and meringues we went out to see what the city had in the way of nightlife. They seem to have quite a bit. We went from café to night-club and finally ended up in the "Parisina" a low place which had plenty of drink and a first class cabaret show. I met a charming gal (a blonde) called Marie. She was very attractive and danced very well. Afterwards we went back to our hotel (just Dick & I) as they have a curfew at 12 PM everything closes at 11.

The next day, Saturday, we departed 2:30 back for camp and lost our way I was in the back and Dick in front. When I took over I found we were heading for Germany so I quickly stopped and after a lot of bother got back on the right road. It took 6½ hours to get back.

Well I enjoyed it. I must say but there was nothing to eat for 48 hours which rather dampened the festive spirit. But I must also say I haven't seen any town so like peace time since 1939. One could get almost any luxury (at a price) watches – leather goods – perfumes – clothes – sweets – meringues (lovely) – ice cream and loads of whipped cream 'licious bags of fruit but no solid food like meat, butter, eggs etc. At night also it was just like peacetime. All the lights up and coloured signs dancing and cabarets plenty to drink though no whiskey or gin but then they never did go for that much did they.

Well that is a picture of Brussells and I hope to get a chance to visit it again. Though under better arrangements.

Did I make your mouth water, it did mine. I spent 2,500 francs 750 on perfumes 1,025 on wine for the Company Mess. So you can see it's pretty expensive 126 to 1 pound.

......Goodbye Baba dearest and tons and tons of love. I was lucky yesterday (Sunday) to get to confession and communion. Thank you for all the prayers

From Peter xxxxxxx

Tuesday 17th October

We are on the move again ("Once more into the breach, dear friends" etc.). All morning was spent packing up pl kit and getting ready. Then we went. Barney is making a recce [reconnaisance] of the area to be taken over. After hanging about in the cold we moved off at 12 and were taken to the bridge at Nijmegen to guard it.

We have to live in the base of the bridge itself. Dog Rough!! Couple of Jerry's ME109 [Messeschmitt Bf109 fighter aircraft] came over nothing much happened.

Wednesday 18th October

Quite a bit of shelling. Terrific alertness to be maintained. Reports of submarines coming down the river kept everyone bobbing. Commanding Officer round last night helluva temper. Another report of a man on a raft. Things look damn funny. However nothing materialises save the odd shells. The duties are damn tiring 2 on and 4 off but only 3hrs sleep for one I'm afraid.

Thursday 19th October

More blasted shelling during the night. Have decided to cook for ourselves. Everyone bobbing a lot including me (trying to keep out of mischief).

Got some mail which is welcome. There are no lights at all here a few candles have to suffice. Have found some smashing pears.

Friday 20th October

Get relieved today by No4 Coy. Dennis took over. We marched back to a school with hot baths and electric lights what comfort! Robin, Paddy and I share a room. Had a lovely bath in the afternoon.

A dance this evening – Not too good, too many civilians but rather good listening to dance band again.

Saturday 21st October
Spent in 'lapping it up'. Its good to get a nights rest once again.

Sunday 22nd October
Went to Mass and Communion
Edward went off to Brussels today. Barney bobbing like hell over taking over the bridge tomorrow. Poor old B.

Monday 23rd October
Took over at eleven from D. [Dennis]. All quiet until evening. The shells whizzed.

Tuesday 24th October
Shelling at dawn and had to go to command post while Barney went to C.O.s. Pl killed one sheep today which tasted very nice.
During stand to at 1900hrs a blinking shell landed 20 yds away wasn't touched hope luck keeps with me. Poor old Paddy broke his ankle last night fell down a drop. Tough luck.

Wednesday 25th October
Major General supposed to be coming tomorrow terrific flap on everyone bobbing as normal. I had to issue bags of orders.

Thursday 26th October
Handed over to Rupert's platoon he was in Brussells lucky dog but will arrive tonight. Marched back to the good old school and comfort. Had a welcome bath and changed. Barney to Brussells.

Friday 27th October
Went on 'lapping it up' but had to attend course in Clothing and Winter Woollies. Listened to a gdsm in No.4 Coy play swing all evening.

To: Mrs P.H. Morrissey
        11 Wilberforce Road, Southsea Hants

No1 Coy
3rd Battalion Irish Guards
B.L.A
27th October [1944]

Baba darling,

Here is a short letter just to let you know I am still fine I'm still hoping that blasted war will be over soon. I must say though it certainly looks as if there is going to be a winter campaign and I am not looking forward to that.

... Did I tell you that in my platoon I have a professional butcher and cook which as you can realise is a great asset. For every time we go to the front or are on our own. The platoon eats extremely well! Last time we had 3 sheep which I may add does just about 2 days!! I had the biggest chop I have ever seen, and some lovely roast leg. Of course one is always covered from awkward questions by the fact that the sheep are wounded and then bought by the platoon if there are any questions!!!

... I told the Adjutant I didn't want to stay in the army after the war so that's that! I think I can change my mind if necessary. But I don't honestly want to stay in. Only what to do I'm not quite sure. What about the B.O.A. [British Overseas Airways] do you think Tim could help there? Or have you any other ideas? If I stay in the army I will have to stay in for five years and will most probably have to go to Japan which, much as I realise the necessity, I don't relish the idea at all. And even if I didn't go out there I should still have to get a job at 28 unless I made it permanent and it will never be paying concern will it!?

I must close now but will write again as soon as poss.

Goodbye and tons and tons of love

From your loving son Peter xxxxx

To: Wren Patricia Morrissey W.R.N.S.
        11 Wilberforce Road, Southsea Hants

No1 Coy
3rd Battalion Irish Guards
B.L.A
27th October [1944]

Patricia darling,

... Dear, dear, dear life is very much "browning off" at present. I
expect you know I was very pleased about being in Edward Fisher-
Rowe's Company. Well I didn't know him then but now I don't see
how it could possibly be in a worse company. My dear! he is simply
awful. The most unsociable, selfish and conceited man I think I
have ever met. Of course one might get to like him but I'm afraid
he is not my idea of even a good Coy Commander. And it is the
same with the other officers. They think the same thing exactly so
life is very difficult as it's bad enough normally. But when you come
out of the line for a rest you want a pleasant officer commanding
you or else you begin to feel downhearted.

However we just have to put up with it. The cardigan hasn't turned
up but I sure would like a pair of khaki gloves please, can you
manage it thank you? Must write to my fond Mama now so please
excuse and tons and tons of love from your loving brother Peter
XXX

P.S. could you also send me a cigarette holder? sorry

Saturday 28th October

Robin goes to Brussells wrote six letters and received quite a few.

Poor Patrick was killed during our stay here by a A/P Bomb. Awfully unlucky RIP.

Moved to billets for a rest only been there two days when we had to move back on the Bridge. Took back from the Welsh Guards and what a filthy mess they left the place in – they are off to Sittard.

Went on bridge again and this time I was reserve platoon and had a 'cushy' job.

Whilst we were here four of my platoon who had gone "flying" came back and were put in arrest. During one afternoon a shell hit Bn H.Q. and took the leg off one of them and wounded another.

Shelling of Bn H.Q. and School area rather heavy. Quite a few casualties and wounded.

46

CHAPTER 4
NOVEMBER '44

By November the war resolved itself into a slow hard slog in appalling conditions. Progress would be minimal until the spring when the front-lines could be better supplied and supported with artillery. Their offensive in the Ardennes had given the Germans time to consolidate their defences along the Rhine, only sixty miles in front of the Allied lines.

The Battalion found itself holding an area some 20 miles north of Maastricht. Their worst enemy was probably the weather. To counter any further German advance, the Battalion was sent back into Belgium, halfway between Brussels and Maastricht, to a place called Landen where they could be used for a counter-attack, should one be necessary.

It was on 15th November during a reconnaissance of the part of the line that No I Company was to hold that Robin O'Kelly was killed. For the rest of the month the Battalion held this sector of the line and were subjected to a certain amount of shelling. There was patrolling on both sides and the Battalion came out of the line on 1st December.

To: Captain (s) Morrissey M.B.E. R.N.
        Royal Navy Barracks, Portsmouth, Hants

No2 Coy
3rd Battalion Irish Guards
B.L.A
4th November [1944]

My dearest Pat,

... Did I ever tell you about my driver? As you most probably know we have a T.C.V. (troop carrying vehicle) for a platoon to move around in sometimes. And I have a special one all the time. Well that driver is approximately 4 feet nothing and his shoulders come up to the top of one wheel. So that with ease he can put his head over the wheel and look underneath the T.C.V. it looks the most ridiculous thing you ever saw.

My word but I am simply furious and shall be for some time. The Coy Comdr Edward decided to be a bit sociable for a change and invited the Commanding Officer to dinner plus a couple of "big hats" from the Brigade. But during the afternoon he sent for Robin O'Kelly and myself and suggested we had our dinner in private and in other words kicked us out of our own mess as far as the dinner was concerned I didn't care two monkey's tails, but the way Edward, an ex-schoolmaster treated the two platoon commanders I think was disgraceful. We felt just like small boys being sent out of the room because some grown-ups were coming to dinner. What a life!! I thought in a Service Battalion everyone was far gayer and merrier but really we might just as well be back in the Training Battalion.

But there I go complaining so I'd better stop and close. I only hope things will get better soon. Give my love to Baba and tell her I am writing to her. She should have received a letter from me written yesterday. By the way don't do too much work !! Or am I being too optimistic.

Cheerio Capt(s) and Tons and Tons

of love from your loving son Peter xxxx

Sunday 12th November
Handed over to Canadians as this army is to stretch from Nijmegen to the Sea. We are off at 1600hrs on an all night run to Sittard area.

Monday 13th November
Arrived at a place called Grevenbicht about 0800hrs. Into some damn good billets – I lost 74 G. (£6) at 'shute'.
Left for Brussells at 1300hrs. Arrived at 1630hrs and stayed in the Div. Club there.

Tuesday 14th November
Arose at 1200hrs!!
Saw a film in the afternoon.
Went dancing in evening.

Wednesday 15th November
Had lunch at Officers Club (Naafi)
Left B. 1400hrs
Arrived back to Billets about 5 to find whole Bn gone up on to the line.
Chased up after them and heard that early in the afternoon (2.P.M) a shell had caught Robin – Shane – Sgt. McMahon, Sgt. Kettle, Sgt. Bereick, Grogan and 2 others.
Robin and Sgt McMahon died in the evening RIP
Poor Robin he was extremely popular with everybody.

Thursday 16th November
Took up my position as No 1 Pl Comd.
Went out on a recce patrol shells and mortars came over dozens of them. Some very near misses.

Friday 17th November
Big lot of mail today.
More shells too. All Canadians have packed up and gone.

Poor Sgt. Allen ran into a booby trap and got his right leg filled with shrapnel,
We are in a place called Nieuwstadt. N. of Sittard.

Saturday 18th November
Terrific lot of gun fired during the night, ours I'm glad to say.

* * *

To: Captain (S) Morrissey M.B.E. R.N.
        11 Wilberforce Road, Southsea Hants

No1 Coy
3rd Battalion Irish Guards
B.L.A
20th November [1944]

My dearest Pat,

... I won't rise to the bait accept to say that I'd like to see the Sailor who can march past in anyway nearly as good as a Guardsman. Mind you I'm not saying they don't turnout well. But their job is entirely different to ours and they just can't help it, but nine out of ten have a load on their shoulders all the time.

My! But when we are out here we live rather well, at times, when we are left as a platoon to our own resources. Especially if we are in the line. Then the countryside supplies the little dainties and extras that she cannot get back behind. Once we had six chickens; and when I first came out and we were occupying a position quite close to the enemy we killed about six sheep and a couple of calves (we have a professional butcher in my platoon – very handy). You can imagine how we lived then. I used to have roast lamb chops about two or three at a time. One of the chickens we killed was dead minus its head but it would not lie down. It kicked about and flapped its wings around without a head. A truly ludicrous sight. Then the Dutch folk all have masses of bottled fruit in their cellars and of course if you are up in the forward position and the house is subject to shell fire then there's no point in leaving all the glorious fruit (raspberries, plums, cherries, etc.) so we just help ourselves. This is known as liberating livestock.

I'm back now where I started just Edward the 2nd i/c [Second in Command] and myself. Paddy Higgins broke his ankle and Shane Jaimeson got wounded and poor Robin got killed R.I.P. as a matter of fact the 2 i/c wasn't with us when I started. Our original 2 i/c went to another Coy.

Well, Pat, what a war! Surely the Hun will crack soon. But, to be sure, it doesn't look like it from out here. I wish to God they would, and let us all get some peace. By the way if you are thinking of sending me another sweater can you get a polar neck please. It doesn't matter about it being khaki that's not necessary. And if you will let me know how much I'll send a cheque as I must have quite a balance now.

I will write again soon.

Give everyone my love and loads of love to you

from Peter XXX

To: Mrs P.H. Morrissey
        11 Wilberforce Road, Southsea Hants

                                            No1 Coy
                            3rd Battalion Irish Guards
                                              B.L.A
                          21st November [1944]

Baba Darling,

... Poor little Robin was killed the other day by a shell R.I.P. I was extremely sorry as he was one of my best friends. It's terrible when your friends, people you've known for a long time get killed he was only just 20 too. He was at Ampleforth with me. I got the Ampleforth journal alright last night. I will write a short letter to Fr. Terrence sometime soon.

... Loads and loads of love

from Peter XXX

P.S. if you are getting me another sweater can you get a polar neck one please?!

CHAPTER 5
DECEMBER '44

December on the whole was an uneventful month, spent for the most part by both Battalions in the area of Attenhoven. The breakthrough in the Ardennes caused a certain amount of activity, as brilliantly portrayed in the series 'Band of Brothers', and the battalions were moved to a position of readiness. Apart from guarding for a short time some bridges over the Meuse against saboteurs, they were not called on and everyone was gathered together for Christmas Day, which was a great success.

There is a break in my father's diary entries until February 1945, but he continued to write letters home and the events of Christmas Day are well documented in the Regimental history as follows:

Christmas Day was bright. At eleven o'clock there was a special High Mass, with a choir of children dressed in hideous white frocks. Then the two battalions sat down together to dinners. The pioneers covered the desks with boards and found a bottomless store of lanterns and garlands. "Christmas dinners always seem to get larger every year, and this year's wallop of tinned turkey, roast pork, roast beef, boiled potatoes, fried potatoes, peas, cabbage, brussels sprouts and plum puddings had to be seen to be believed. The tables groaned under the beer, cigars, cigarettes and chocolate ration."

No1 Coy
3rd Battalion Irish Guards
B.L.A
1st December [1944]

My Darling Baba,

......We are in some fine billets at present and I got me a splendid mansion with a lovely bedroom. Everyone around here is Catholic and the houses are crammed full of holy pictures – crucifixes – statues. Our Catholic Sergeant said to me "You can't get into bed for the holy pictures and statues in the room." However it's a good thing I'm very glad to see it. It makes up for the rest of Holland which is Protestant. Thanks so much for sending off the parcels to les girls. They both arrived quite safely. What a pity about the radio. Still perhaps it's going now. I heard the news today for the first time for quite a while and it sounded rather good. Though I'm not sure I like the idea of a winter over here but I'm afraid we are resigned to the fact now. It seems so absurd when we were actually in Germany at one point doesn't it. It's most unlike the Hun to keep on fighting. The answer is I think this unconditional surrender. He sure is going to fight hard when that's all he's got to look forward to. What about this 'em battleship wot is big I suppose you all know its name and everything about it. It certainly sounds quite a feather in our naval cap. I got a grand letter from mother and daughter Virginia. And I've got the cutest little lamb in blue wool with a bell round its neck for my godchild to cut her eleven teeth on. The toys over here are simply wonderful so I just couldn't miss the chance. I think I'll send it direct. Received another letter from Patricia ce soir. So I must write her a line. At last we managed to get some whiskey (great stuff-whiskey!) and I got a bottle all to myself. 8/6 good don't you think? Hope to get some more tomorrow. This afternoon I took a truck and motored into the Fatherland but found it pretty much the same as Holland.

I hope to get to Mass tomorrow and the Sacraments it is really quite a long time since I've had the chance. Dear Edward has become quite genial at last so much so that I can't quite make it out. He got rid of Barney, whom he couldn't get on with and now Billy Reynolds is back with us. So we are in the same position when I joined the Coy. Which is rather good but I would like another platoon commander for company as both Billy and Edward are pretty ancient compared to me. However someone will come out soon I'm sure. Goodbye and all my love and I will write as often as I can. Lots and lots of love from your loving Peter XXX

Baba darling

Here are a few Christmas presents for the family and one for Barbara could you give them out please. I do hope they don't take too long to reach you. The box was the only one I could find anywhere.

I do hope you have a perfectly wonderful Christmas. I'll be thinking of you. Everything's fine here so don't worry. Lots and lots of love to you all

from your loving son

Peter

Excuse paper please. Yes?

To: Mrs P.H. Morrissey
        11 Wilberforce Road, Southsea Hants

No1 Coy
3rd Battalion Irish Guards
B.L.A
8th December [1944]

My darling Baba,

Terribly sorry I haven't been able to write for such an age but I did actually pencil a letter a few days back only I couldn't send it off so I am writing this now to you as we have a better chance for a day or two of being able to get off our mail. Gosh! What a place I've never seen so much mud in all my days! Still we comfort ourselves with the fact that if it it's bad for us then by George it must be too awful for Jerry. After all we have something to look forward to but the Hun must know he's beaten and therefore he has nothing at all to look forward to. And judging by four who came over to my position a few days back and gave themselves up I say they were pretty fed up now. The only thing keeping them going being the S.S. and Gestapo troops. Perhaps I'm being optimistic but I'm certain that sooner or later they will crack and I think sooner rather than later. Still as I say perhaps I'm being too optimistic! I hope I'm right though.

Baba, right now, there is a radio in the room and it's making me feel so homesick it's playing "All the things you are" remember it? Before the war I think. Anyway it's pretty good finding a radio in these parts. This one is a good pre-war one which has been buried for 3 years!

... I sent off a parcel to you all with all my love for Christmas. I do hope it makes it alright. And two lots of Christmas cards. Let me know if everything turns up will you please? There is a watch for Cherub but not in the parcel. I'm sending that off pronto but it will take a little extra time. I am so glad the other parcel arrived and was alright.

We now have two more officers William Moore and Claude Proby whom I don't think you know. Let's hope they have better luck. I'm glad to see the Navy have a good Battleship. I think the Americans will go all out to beat it don't you? Do you know her name I wonder.

... Loads and loads of love from your loving son Peter XXX

CHAPTER 6
JANUARY '45

The 3rd Battalion spent January 1945 in Atenhoven and Landen being well cared for by the locals and enjoyed an almost peacetime routine of training which was described as 'uneventful'. They were however blissfully unaware as to what lay ahead of them just a few weeks hence.

This period is again aptly described in *A History of The Irish Guards in The Second World War* as follows:

> *For once they were able to watch the war progressing cleanly and quietly in chinagraph across the map. As a further consolation, the Home Leave scheme started almost according to plan. In true democratic fashion lots were drawn and the lucky few who got the first places actually went. A fortnight later they returned with news from England and reports of the damage done by Vs. 1 and 2 in London, which up to now had been the German prisoners' favourite topic of conversation.*
>
> *But social life occupied most of the days. Visits to Brussels were easy and as frequent as finance allowed. A lucky few even went to Paris on business or compassionate grounds. Landen and Atenhoven, too, did their best to be gay with their parties, dances and the village hospitality.*

To: Mrs P.H. Morrissey
        11 Wilberforce Road, Southsea Hants

No1 Coy
3rd Battalion Irish Guards
B.L.A
3rd January[1945]

My darling Baba

… I am so glad D. is back again at the grindstone as it's no good him being ill especially as he has only just been promoted and anyhow I'm sure he prefers to be up and about. Is lying in bed – The Idle Man that he is! I told you the polar sweater arrived and was received most gratefully. Thank you so much! My word the Hun is taking a terrific cracking these days. Let's hope he completely cracks. I think he may, and anyhow it's better to be optimistic don't you think? Listening to the news about the 1,000 bomber daylight raid on Berlin 2,000 tonnes in ¾ of an hour. Not bad !!

… Thank heavens the weather has at last changed for the better. At any rate the snow has disappeared. I expect it is pretty much the same back in old England. Almost overnight the snow thawed out. And now the sun comes out all day. The only thing being that it tends to change the ground into a seething churned up mass of mud. Still one can't have the best time and Lord knows what is the best.

Have you been having anymore gay times lately? Plenty of parties is always the thing to keep up the spirit I sure would like to be back home now and help you out with one.

… By the way I saw "Eddie Cantor" in show business the other day and really enjoyed it. It wasn't frightfully original but at the same time it was song and dance and rather amusing. By far the best one I've seen since I came out was Home in Indiana in glorious technicolour!! I must say that film book you sent me for Christmas has proved very valuable as I have been able to check up on films I have seen advertised and find out quite a lot about them. And thank you for the two "Picture Goers" which have so far turned up.

Well Baba "Any day now!" I suppose is the slogan in England at present and I think perhaps it may be right but give it three good weeks or so. Then Heigh-Ho for Burma! But first a spot of leave is indicated don't you think? Please don't worry Baba about me if I am not able to keep up a regular mail. As I have told you we don't always get the chance to write a lot. Must close now and all the best lots and lots of love from Peter.

To: Mrs P.H. Morrissey
        11 Wilberforce Road, Southsea Hants

No1 Coy
3rd Battalion Irish Guards
B.L.A
14th Jan [1945]

Baba darling,

... Well, we had a big "do" here last night. We held a company-squadron dance that is to say No1 company and No1 Squadron 2nd Bn got a hall and a certain amount of drink and a damn good band, from the Battalion, and we put up a dance. It was all rather fun except that the girls were very few and far between. It's absolutely extraordinary but they refused to come 1. without a chaperone and 2. without a written invitation in both French and English. The local Padre of the village was broached on the subject by Fr. Hartington. And he positively refused to have anything to do with it. Anyway we held it despite everything and when it was going full swing the lights suddenly went out all over the town and so there was rather chaos. However we continued with candle power, and all the officers retired to our mess where we drank Martell Brandy and sang rude songs. Altogether a highly entertaining evening was had by all. (must go to church now 11 AM will continue afterwards).

Rather good mass which actually didn't start until 11:30 and the church here is not the warmest place by a long way. My poor old "tabs" were frozen. I have thought you might like an account of my doings since I left England and I think up to a certain time I am allowed to tell you. Anyway it's not much but here it is:

I left Southampton on a sunny day and steamed down to the Isle of Wight where we lay off for the night, so close to Portsmouth and yet so far. At approx. 7.30 the following morning we sailed, we were in four American destroyers and all 4 were in line ahead. The first part of the crossing was a little rough but the sun stayed out and the trip was quite pleasant. Towards four o'clock we sighted land and very soon afterwards we were safe up alongside one of the landing stages brought across from England on "D" day. On disembarking we marched to Bayeux and camped outside in tents. We stayed here for nearly a week, while up at the front Brussels was being taken and the Armoured Division had reached the Escaut Canal. Here, as you may know they were stopped for about 3 weeks.

We next started our journey across France which took another week for we had to stay at R.H.U.s on the way (Reinforcement Holding Units). The train, which was the first one to make the journey, was interminably slow and at one particular point the fireman let the fire out and we had to wait for the steam to be raised again. As the train stopped every 20 minutes or so, for 20 minutes, all the men used to get off and pick apples from the orchards on either side of the track and consequently when the train started again there was the most terrific scramble to get back on again and once when myself and an officer in the Scots Guards were some 100 yds from the train it started off and I can tell you, it took a good deal of running to catch up with the last coach and jump aboard.

We arrived at a small station outside Brussels and went to another R.H.U. After a couple of days there we went to a Divisional Transit Camp and by this time the Battalion had broken out of Escaut and captured Joe's Bridge and Eindhoven and was steaming to Nijmegen. Here it was that we watched the 1st Parachute Battalion go over to Arnhem. Truly a wonderful sight. The sky was black with aircraft and it was very thrilling indeed to watch them. Our departure was put off by the fact that the Hun had cut the main road into Holland just above Eindhoven. This meant that the Armoured Division was cut off and very little else was with it.

For a while then things looked pretty black but luckily the Germans were pushed back off the road, and though were still able to shell it, and did, the road was once again clear.

So we set off. A big convoy of troops, badly wanted reinforcements, driven by volunteer drivers whose job was one of driving tanks. Just outside Eindhoven my driver ditched the truck but managed to pull himself out. No sooner had he pulled himself out than he ran into the ditch again, then this time for good. The time was 2030 hours and the light was failing fast. Here was I then with twenty Irish Reinforcements and a ditched T.C.V. still some fifty kilometres to go and not really having any idea where to go to.

After holding a council with the drivers we decided that the best thing to do in fact the only thing, was for the men to get some sleep and in the morning I would walk back into Eindhoven and try and procure a breakdown gang to pull us out. So in the field by the side of the road the Guardsmen tried to sleep. The night was bitterly cold and seemed to pass very slowly. One or 2 German planes came over and were shot at. But nothing else happened. Myself and a Sergeant stayed awake all night – it was the only way to keep warm.

At last the dawn broke and leaving the men to light a fire Sergeant Rennold and I set off to Eindhoven. Here we luckily found a relief outfit who came out and finally got the T.C.V out of the ditch. The convoy, of course, had departed soon after we had been deposited in the ditch the previous night. So we were on our own and consequently able to make good speed.

Coming into a small town Vilno [close to Uden] half way between Eindhoven and Nijmegen my driver, who unfortunately kept imagining himself back in a tank ran straight into a carrier and completely broke the front left hand spring, which of course finished the T.C.V. By good fortune we had this accident near the 1st Motorised Grenadiers who had incidentally been sent back to deal with the break in the road, and after I had been to see them they very obligingly lent me two half tracks with which to finish the journey. With fresh heart we set off and reached Nijmegen at about 6 that evening cross the bridge with the odd shell sent over by Jerry to help us on our way.

So we arrived. The Battalion had had a pretty nasty set back and the 2nd had lost a few tanks. I deposited the men at Bn Headquarters and joined Edward in No1 Coy. That night the bridge was heavily attacked. The noise was terrific, I heard William McFetridge had been killed R.I.P. No.1 Coy No1 squadron was sharing a mess in a collaborators home five kilometres from Nijmegen bridge. The "line" was five kilometres further up the road...

I must end now Baba dearest I hope you find it interesting and I will continue in the next letter.

Lots and lots of love from Peter XXX

P.S. We are putting on French drama here for Saint Patrick's Day I have a part!

To: Mrs P.H. Morrissey
         11 Wilberforce Road, Southsea Hants

No1 Coy

3rd Battalion Irish Guards

B.L.A

27th January [1945]

My Dearest Baba,

... Patricia seems to have started her course in the approved Morrissey style, 20 minutes adrift. Still I'm sure she will do splendidly. Only she must get her hat the right size and not one of those ridiculous looking small size ones or too large. Remember at K.A. when we went to that play?

Talking of the play that's the one we are putting on here or rather hope to for St Patrick's Day. We will all learn our parts and then at the right moment and given a little freedom from shells will gather the Bn somewhere and put it on. I believe Fr. Hartington has laid on a girl from Brussels a C.W.L. [Catholic Women's League] girl to take the leading female part. It will be fun getting it up even if it doesn't ever come off.

... I managed to serve mass this morning.

CHAPTER 7
FEBRUARY '45: 'OPERATION VERITABLE'

A History of The Irish Guards in The Second World War goes on to record the following.

> *While the Americans were slowly pushing the Germans out of the Ardennes, the Guards Armoured Division, with most of the 21st Army Group, enjoyed the first real rest since Normandy.*
>
> *By 25th January, 12th Corps, which had relieved the Division in the Geleen-Geilinkirchen sector, had driven the Germans back across the river Roer from Julich to Roermond. The ground was now ready for "Operation Veritable" a grand offensive by the 21st Army Group to clear the Germans from the left (west) bank of the Rhine. On 5th February the Guards Armoured Division followed the rest of 30th Corps north to Tilburg.*
>
> *On 8th February one of the biggest artillery barrages of the war began.*

Name	Rk.	Reg No	Rel	AGE	Single	Children / family
1/Buckley A.	Sgt.	2718277	C.I	28	married	Nil
Casey D.		2422816	R.C.	32	married	Nil
Gannon T.	L/Sgt	2721365	R.C.	33	married	one
Halford B.	L/Cpl	2721280	R.C.	23	married	one
Denny W.	L/Cpl	2724296	C.E	21	Single	—
Doggart J.	"	2723997	Pres	21	Single	—
Fallon J.	"	2721738	R.C.	31	married	one
IRVING J.	L/Sgt	2720994	CE	25	married	—
[Kane] J.	L/Cpl	2714050	R.C.	36	married	—
Stocker N.	L/Cpl	14664969	C.E.	29	married	one
Bridge J.	Cdn	2422086	C.E	33	married	two
Carpenter H	"	2724471	C.E.	19	Single	—
Charlton K.	"	2724351	C.E	19	Single	—
[Poulton] C.	"	2724388	C.E	19	Single	—
Davies N.	"	2724396	C.E	19	Single	—
File P.	"	2724332	C.E	20	Single	—
Giles G.	"	2724458	C.E	31	married	one
Jackman G.	"	2424246	R.C	18	Single	—
Kelly B.	"	2724321	R.C.	24	Single	—
Nicollette.	"	2724341	R.C.	19	Single	nil
Murphy N.	"	2724429	C.E.	19	Single	nil

Next of Kin	ADDRESS
Wife	c/o Bonzor, 58 High St. Hawick nr Scotland
wife	20 Lord Mayors walk York England
wife	16 Cooper St Horwich Lancs.
wife	50 Severus Avenue York.
mother	Mrs W.C. Denny Thopewood Farm. Corstoastle Northants
Father	H. Appal 130 Roslyn St. Belfast Co Antrim, Ireland.
wife	10 Council Terrace E Grinstead Sx.
wife	18 Victoria Rd Collbridge Nr Wigan Lancs.
wife	27. Crescent Grove Clapham London S.W4
wife	8, Seymore place Totnes Devonshire
wife	50, La Glendse St Bolton, Lancs.
mother	3. Bowerman Rd. Chadwell St Mary nr Grays
mother	Mrs R. Charkworth 7. Longcroft Grove. Royal Oak Est Estate Wythenshawe Manchester.
mother	Mrs H. Conkie Spurstowe Hall Cottages Bunbury Tarporley Cheshire
mother	Mrs L. Davies The Green Wrenbury near Nantwich Cheshire
mother	SA. 10 Braid Avenue East Acton London W
wife	47 Southchurch Rd Eastham London E. 6
Father	C. 9. Burr Rd Southfields wandsworth London s.w
Sister	M. ATS Record Office Winchester Hants.
mother	M. 8 main St Howth Co Dublin Eire
Father	F. 125 Somers Rd Southsea Portsmouth

6th February – 5th March
Move from Landen to Tilburgh was accomplished on
Tuesday 6th February. A tiring journey but some excellent
billets reached at the end. Masses of flying bombs sent over.
Attack by 7 Divs [7th Armoured Division] went in Thursday
we have to wait till Cleves falls we are still waiting.
Everything is packed up and ready. The weather is perfectly
appalling

<u>**Exercise Veritable**</u>
February 10th Saturday
Tilburgh still waiting to move. Possible we might move
during the night. Though things are going extremely well.
The weather seems to be holding up the advance. Rain this
morning but the sky cleared this afternoon and the sun came
out. (Got a Valentine Card from someone.) Everyone very
optimistic but we all hate this waiting.

To: Mrs P.H. Morrissey
        11 Wilberforce Road, Southsea Hants

No1 Coy
3rd Battalion Irish Guards
B.L.A
10th February [1945]

My darling Baba and Pat,

... Talking of weather it has cleared up quite a lot but unfortunately now pours with rain thus the ground is slowly being turned into a sea of churned up mud. It's so bad we can't have really first class weather to finish off the war. The Russians seem to be forging ahead and perhaps we will do the same. Did you get my letter by courier I wonder. I sent it home by Frankie who was going on leave. By the way I never said I would be home in March I don't even expect to be. It only means that my 6 months overseas is up then and after that it may way a couple of months and most likely more before I get off as only about 2 officers per battalion get leave each month. Some who have been over here since "D" day still haven't had their date yet. And unless this war is finished quickly and then the leave is speeded up quite a bit, I honestly can't see myself home till late summer. No I really would rather this thing was finished first and then get home as the ones who have already had their's don't feel too happy on returning.

... I do hope the Buzz Bombs and Rockets aren't bothering you nowadays. They send them over us TFO (till further orders). Most thank heavens, go over but the odd one comes down somewhere near at hand and then everything rattles and trembles. I filled up my flask, remember it, with some White Horse whiskey today it should come in handy it has already. Once whilst we were holding the line I filled it with some whiskey and left it by mistake on the table of my pl. HQ. When I next saw it, it had been emptied and thrown to one side so I didn't get much benefit out of that!

I'll write again as soon as possible keep your fingers crossed and say a prayer for me. We had general absolution and Holy Communion the other day and I went to mass yesterday morning. I must close now so lots and lots of love to you both all my love Peter

* * *

February 11th Sunday
Moved off from Tilburgh at 14:15 hrs No1 Coy leading. Via H'bosh. Rain started here and then poured solidly all day. Arrived about 6pm at Nijmegen. Weather perfectly appalling. Never have I seen such rain and mud. The Coy is mostly Billeted in a hospital. No 1 Pl has a barn of its own. The guns are banging away and it is snowing.

February 12th Monday
A fine morning. Dry and chilly. The Coy is in a hospital No1 Pl in a barn and things not too bad. The cook house rather good. Rain came on in the evening. A bit of a hoax had on me tonight (to give a lecture).

February 13th Tuesday
Move order came through for Coy to move to Grosebech. Everything packed up and Coy left at 12.45. A grand day and everyone in good spirits. Arrived at "G" a Dutch Village on the border absolutely smashed up, each pl in a house, rain came on in the evening. Whilst having dinner. Edward called to "O" [Orders] group. Came back and told us we were to attack as I. [Infantry] Brigade tomorrow on Geneppe. What fun! Champagne to boot!

February 14th Wednesday
Moved off from "G" 10am and arrived outside Geneppe. Actual place we are to attack is Hommersum. The Colys

[Coldstream Guards] are putting in an attack first to gain a high ridge. Then with No1 Coy left, No3 Coy right the Bn will attack next village.

At 1330 hrs after a feed the Bn moves off. Concentrated behind the Colys while a 20 min barrage went down. The Colys attacked and won their ridge and we moved up into position. As soon as the barrage started for us we moved off down the hill and across the open country. The barrage was tremendous! My pl was up on the right. Willies on the left. We reached the houses this side of the village and cleared them, then "bounced" the bridge into the village itself. Cleared more houses and dug in. Had to move on about five hundred yds to some farm buildings we made the pl area! Got dug in just in time before Jerry opened up on us with all he'd got -The worst part of any attack is the heavy counter attack by fire by the enemy.

Willie's Pl got caught up by a railway bridge which was blown. However he managed to get across and capture 4 Spandaus [German machine gun] and about 20 men. Then he came up to the farm buildings.

Pretty quiet night. A good load of mail came up for me.
It has been a simply marvellous day.

Thursday 15th Feb

A patrol of 3 Coy got wiped out. Nothing much except shells and mortar all morning.

In the afternoon a general "stand-to" as No.2 Coy was being attacked from the South. A patrol of Richard Tenison ran into the counter attack and 2 Coy got badly knocked about. 2pls of 4 Coy had to reinforce them. So under cover of a thick fog (providential) we were able to withdraw to 4 Coy's position.

The counter attack was beaten off and during the night some of the patrol managed to get back including Richard who was wounded. The fog held all night long and some more letters arrived tonight for me. The attack has been a complete success Thank God. But the casualties are estimated around 40. It was held by 300 German troops and the Bn took 150 prisoners. Well done the Micks!

Friday 16 Feb
The day is lovely again, clear blue sky. Odd shells etc. whizz over The Colys are to put in an attack this afternoon. Another terrific barrage goes down and Typhoons and Spits [Spitfires] have a 'field-day'. The Colys gained their objective. The (Welsh Guards are to attack at 5 tomorrow morning) S.P. and flame throwers give the Hun a bit of a bashing and just for fun he takes it out on us – more shells! We help to build a footbridge across railway for the W.G. to cross at approx. 0300hrs. They are attacking Hassum good luck to em. Got a small parcel tonight.

Saturday 17th Feb
The W.G. apparently walked into H without seeing a single Hun and therefore had no casualties. The shells and mortars are slacking off. Heard poor Sgt Mickey Dunne was killed RIP. Not much else happened today Basil B [Basil Berkeley] was also wounded.

Sunday 18 Feb
Have to move pl into another house as Coys are concentrating. The Din of battle has passed away and we gather we are to be rested for a few days. The Coy has opened an Officers Mess and Naffi Packs were issued out today. Things are much better now. Tonight we had a Sgt Mess party. Plenty of meat. Rum was consumed and a hair raising ride back to my pl ended the day.

Monday 19 Feb
Spent most of the day with the pl W. [weapons] Inspection Billets etc. Went for a short walk heard "Goch" had fallen, pretty good effort. Not much resistance, Have to have I.N.C.O. [one non-commisioned officer] and 2 men with 2

L.M.G. [Light Machine Gun] on guard otherwise rest of pl can sleep. Alec & Dennis (R.A) came to dinner. Walked back after dinner to pl building and went to bed. Had Confession & Communion.

Tuesday 20th Feb
Bit of a scare about doing an attack by night but now believe it will be tomorrow. The S.G. [Scotts Guards] are to come up tomorrow about 10 and take over our v.comfortable houses. Went to mass in the shell shattered church of Hommersum. Had Holy Communion. Managed to change my towel and socks. The rains came all day. The mud is perfectly appalling.

* * *

Wednesday 21st Feb [Written by Mickey Morrissey]
    In 'A Tribute' to Major D.M. (John) Kennedy M.C. by Robert Jocelyn the action below was described as follows:
    "'For the first mile or so,' relates the Regimental History, 'the tracks held firm and there was little sign of opposition. Then it started proper. The forward companies ran into mud and mines, and the few carriers that were not blown up got bogged. When the companies were well stuck, the Germans unleashed their guns and mortars. There was a great deal of noise and high explosive, which was not surprising as three German Battalions were holding the area.'
    A senior NCO in one of the Companies remembers the advance well. 'It was a killing ground. We were on the right wing. Mud everywhere. The ditches too deep for vehicles to cross and the two roads mined. Everywhere was littered with mines. Box mines. Teller mines [see glossary]. They were all there. Along the bloody edges of the track – no bigger than this room – were fox holes every fifty yards to cover the mines. And most of them had Spandaus in case the sappers came anywhere near them.'

Numbers 1 and 3 Companies continued to fight their way towards Terporten Castle and Vrig in the realisation that somewhere a terrible mistake had been made. John Kennedy reached the Chateau at the head of the Platoon, Germans streamed out the back door and hopped into trenches. 'Come on lads!' he shouted, 'we've got them now, and running to the trenches in front of everyone else he walked up and down killing Germans with his revolver. He soon used up his ammunition, and was about to jump into a trench when a single shot got him from the flank.

The other Company on the same flank as John had also come under heavy fire. 'It was caught without cover and artillery support. One look at the ground ahead and another at the Guardsmen lying squeezed in the mud was enough to show that it would take a properly supported Battalion to tidy up the village (Vrig) alone. Major Edward Fisher-Rowe had been in every action from Normandy onwards and he was not afraid to make a decision. He ordered No. 1 Company to withdraw to the nearest cover. He saw them started then turned back to pick up the casualties. He and a Guardsman lifted a badly wounded man onto an old gate and carried it down the track. He was killed by a burst of Spandau in the head. Lieutenant Proby and Sergeant Grant, the two forward platoon Commanders, completed the withdrawl.'"

By the time this action took place Colonel Joe Vandeleur had been promoted to take command of a Brigade and Major Basil Eugster M.C. was given command of the Battalion. It was reported that when Joe Vandeluer heard what had happened at Terporten Castle he came rushing up from Brussels and got hold of Major Eugster. 'What have you done to my Battalion!' He shouted at him.

In *A History of The Irish Guards* it states that the Battalion suffered 175 casualties in this attack. 'No doubt great damage was done to the Germans,' wrote an officer, 'but that hardly offset our own losses. The whole thing was much like Sourdeval last summer-the leading companies well-nigh destroyed. We can't afford to lose people like John and Edward and so many first class N.C.O.s and Guardsmen. John had been in fourteen full-scale attacks with the 1st Battalion and ourselves and Edward in everything from Normandy onwards. Both knew their job thoroughly, were loved by their companies and never thought of their own safety. We all know our loss.'

The Guards Armoured Division history mentions that, '...the losses left a bitter taste. Leadership had been excellent and the men had fought superbly; it had just been one of those unlucky days for which nobody could be blamed but which occasionally come in war, often when least expected.' It was not a view universally accepted by those who had fought at Terporten.

* * *

Wednesday 21st Feb
We are to attack today. Leave H. at 1100 and form up along a/Tk [anti-tank] ditch. A lovely day as for the first attack. One Coy up left, 4 Coy up Rt, 3 Coy in rear of 1. 2 in rear of 4. Coy's crossed STpt [start point] at 1300hrs. with a terrific barrage down on houses in front. We advanced, my pl up on Rt, Claude's up on left, across the open fields – The mud & waterlogged country was appalling – About ½ to objective which was "Pleeshof" the Coy was pinned down by Spandau fire. Cpl Kane was killed. Claude did a left flanking attack and captured the houses. My pl established itself in some other houses 20 P.O.W. were taken. Our own mortars were falling very close. The Coy pushed on down the road and came under heavy SP [Spandau] fire from some woods. The country was very thick indeed. The fire was very heavy indeed. The Coy got into a barn and Edward made a plan. Suddenly No.3 Coy on our left in woods started to pull out. A great deal of

Contemporary with legend showing locations as described in the diaries

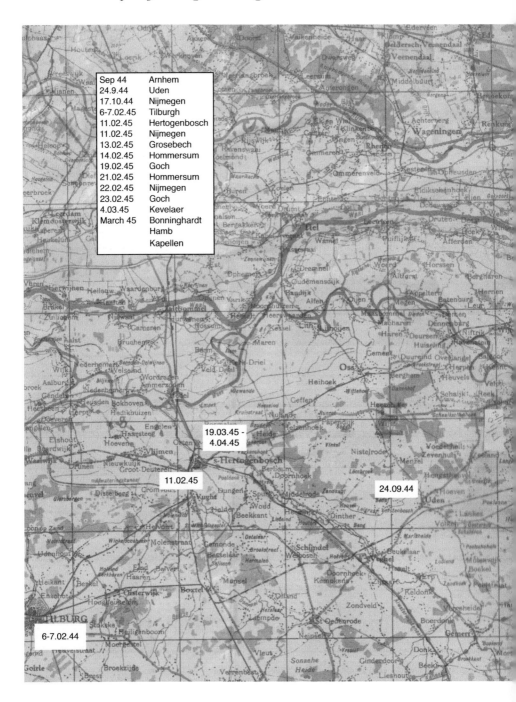

Sep 44   Arnhem
24.9.44   Uden
17.10.44   Nijmegen
6-7.02.45   Tilburgh
11.02.45   Hertogenbosch
11.02.45   Nijmegen
13.02.45   Grosebech
14.02.45   Hommersum
19.02.45   Goch
21.02.45   Hommersum
22.02.45   Nijmegen
23.02.45   Goch
4.03.45   Kevelaer
March 45   Bonninghardt
             Hamb
             Kapellen

19.03.45 -
4.04.45

11.02.45

24.09.44

6-7.02.44

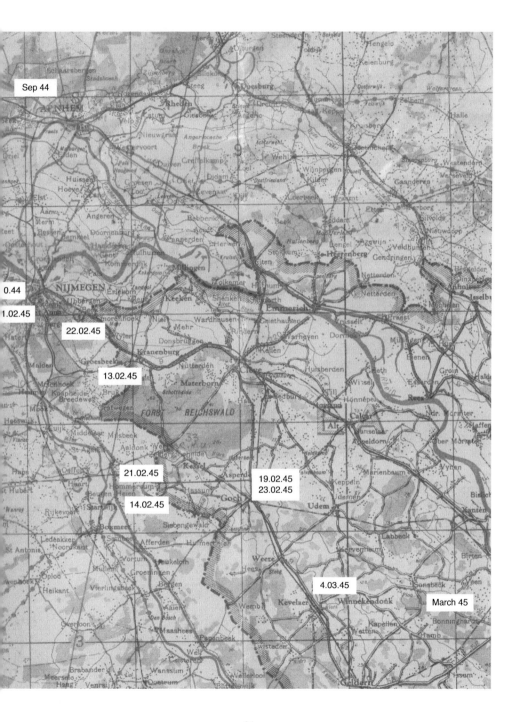

Sep 44

0.44

1.02.45

22.02.45

13.02.45

21.02.45

14.02.45

19.02.45
23.02.45

4.03.45

March 45

81

Battle Map from 1945 centred on Hommersum, complete with battle markings. Note the location of Vrij and Terporten marked on the map. Insert shows battle objective notes.

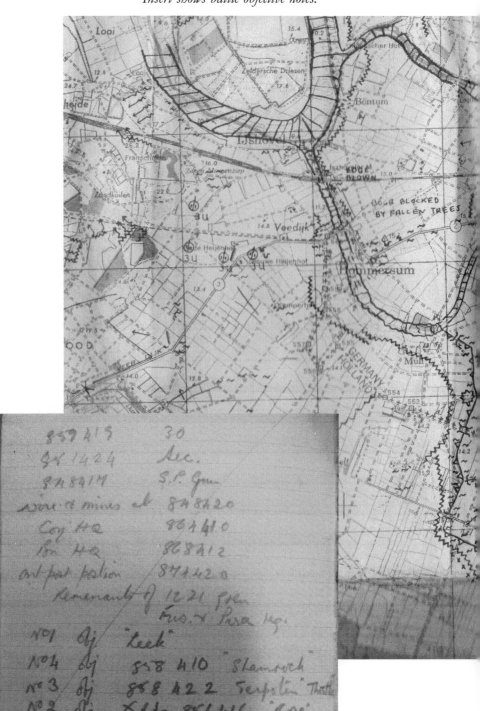

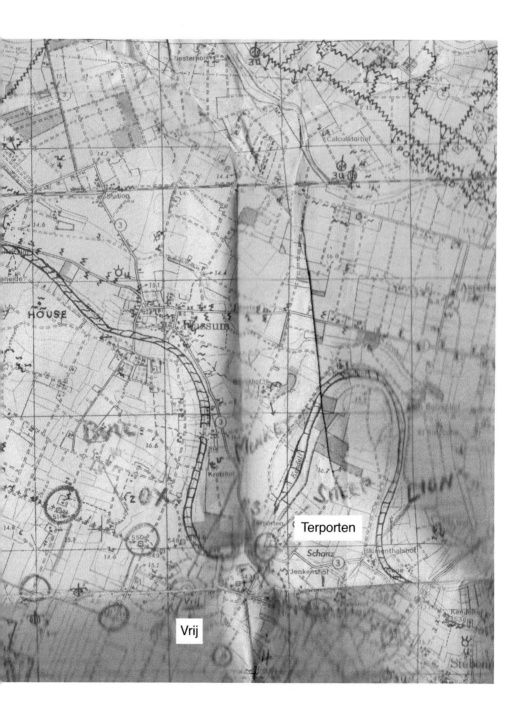

Bn attack

Intention capture Pleeshof 86 41

Fliesagi 88 41

1 up left   4 up Rt

3 back   2 back

Squad 2nd W. B.

4.2 mortar   m/g + Colys m/g

overhead
from left fire

4 m field Reg

4 m

4 Heavies

1 coy attack Pleeshof.

axis of advance. 552 L 550 S. b Rd

1 pl Rt 3 pl left 2 res left

Rate of advance 100x 2 mins

Haversack Rations to be taken

Dress jerkins Equipment Piats. carried

Great Coats to be put on to carrier

Intercom. Tracer + Green V. light

if held up. Red is stop.

w/t

R.A.P. Casualties sent etc back to
start line

assembly area + F.U.P. W of a/tk
ditch st line E. of a/tk ditch
H hour 1300 hrs

Pls ready to move at 10 15
march of 1030
3 coy +a 1 2
Route over bridge past Buitte
Fork left at/ + Turn left 813140
Tools carried
Rev. 6.45
st pt by Church.

4.30 Blankets stacked by Rd junct
extra mortar bombs stacked to carri

return Telephone tesigs.
collect watch from Sgt. Halford

85

smoke came down on us and a frightful barrage Claude's platoon was up on its own trying to deal with the SP [Spandau] fire. There seems to be hundreds of Spandaus all round us and casualties are heavy. Giles, Cpl Denny, Haskel, Jackman, Carpenter and Reed were wounded. Pavey was killed. Edward seeing the situation was getting worse and worse ordered the Coy to retire. First of all the wounded who could walk were taken back and then the pls pulled out my platoon being the last. Giles who was too bad to move had to be put on a door and was carried by four men off down the road. I left. Then Kelly and Edward Left. There was a great deal of SP fire all the time and the place was being heavily shelled and mortared. The smoke was still being put down on top of us. I ran down the lane as fast as I could turned round at the end and saw Edward lying on the ground. Gdsm Kelly came running up and said "The major's been killed sir". Poor Edward, his loss to the Bn is great indeed. A burst of Sp caught him in the back of the neck. R.I.P. Giles had to be left as a shell burst near him and another piece entered his shoulder it was believed to have killed him. The Coy is now grouped around the first objective badly shaken and with many good men lost. We dig in here but are pretty thin on the ground and all our communications have gone. There is no more ammunition left and everyone is pretty dazed and depressed. Here we stay until after dark; the C.O. came up and had a look around. Reports of an enemy tank don't make things any better either. About nine p.m. the remains of the Coy pull out down the road. In single file we set off and as if we hadn't had enough a Junkers came over flying quite low and dropped a couple of bombs nearby.

I don't think they were intended for us but all the same they weren't very pleasant. In this manner the Bn made its way back to the Billet at Hommersum which we had vacated in such high spirits this morning. The Scots Guards who were in our Billets were goodness itself and did everything in their power to make us comfortable. But it has been a very tiring and disheartening day. Casualties are estimated at about 170 men and 8 officers including John Kennedy and Edward. It's not clear what happened to John. It's likely he'll be put in for a V.C. No more now. Only Willie and I remain, Claude who did marvellously and was wounded 3 times has gone back, so many have been lost for so little.

Thursday 22nd Feb
A good rest and some hot food has made all the difference. Never have I been so tired as I was last night. The Coy has to be reorganised. No3 Coy only had 33 men left and no officers. Billy came up and we visited Mick's Coy who only had about 40 men left (no 4) I had to go off on a recce for Billets for the Coy this morning, so left everything and went off with advance party. The Bn is to have a weeks rest to reorganise and try and get up to strength. Having arrived at Nijmegen we are in with the 2nd Bn who are on counter attack role. The Coy arrives and we all get "dug into" some good billets. Drinks with No1 Squadron and then dinner and so to bed.

Friday 23rd Feb
Awoke 0820 to hear 2nd Bn tanks moving off. At 0930 Billy had to go off to make a recce. They are putting us in again to hold the line "No rest for the wicked". I have to put the whole Coy in transport by 1245 when we set off. After a long drive the Bn arrive at a place near Plasdorf N.E.Goch. We drove through outskirts of Goch not much left of Goch from what one can see. The roads the Bn have to get up are too awful. Mud up to axels. Eventually the Coy settles in taking over from the D.C.L.I. [Duke of Cornwall's Light Infantry]. A bit of a change from the taste of luxury we were given in Nijmegen still c'est la Guerre.

Saturday 24th Feb
The Coy is sorting itself out now we have James Osbourne's troop with us. Great "Buzz" of attack going through us. The gun barrage is terrific round here as we have all sorts everywhere. Dennis Fitzgerald is commanding the Bn now. We are to have Chris [Major Chris Dodd] as Coy Commander and Colin Kennard as 2 I/C [Second in Command].

* * *

To: Mrs P.H. Morrissey
       11 Wilberforce Road, Southsea Hants

No1 Coy
3rd Battalion Irish Guards
B.L.A
24th February [1945]

My Dearest Baba and Pat,

... Thank heavens the weather seems to be clearing up at long last. The sun has been shining and it simply wonderful to see all our aircraft in the air. Also the countryside will be usable by tanks and that is a great help. I was awfully pleased to hear Patricia has been raised to the peerage. I expect she looks quite ravishing in her blue and gold. I'm glad you don't think the Japs will prove too much as I shouldn't like to have to go to Burma very much. This has been quite enough for my liking And I don't like this very much. Have you any idea where you might be landed? Malta or perhaps the West Indies I hope I think a job out there would be the thing really.

From your loving son

Peter

Sunday 25th February

Big attack went in through us at 4am, the Barrage was terrific. I missed Mass. Pls are all equipping themselves, very little all day. Sentries as per usual. We have hundreds of German civies round us here. Some are pretty arrogant and need watching.

Monday 26th Feb

Attack going extremely well.

Had mass & H Communion at Bn HQ.

Got a few things for my kit. The news is good from all fronts – No news of our going. They are still trying to find something for us to do.

Tuesday 27th Feb

11 armoured [11th Armoured Division] went in with a swing, all going well T.G.

New men arrived today and the Coy is now up to strength or very nearly. We did a bit of training on tanks and some weapon zeroing. Had mass & Holy Communion in Coy area.

Wednesday 28th Feb

Colin is off and John Fawcus and Brian Russell have joined us. Brian gets Claude's platoon. John is 2 I/C. Willie & I stroll down and have tea with Major Reynolds. The men are road repairing a kit inspection was carried out with the platoons. Whole bunch of Jerries from Uden came in this morning.

CHAPTER 8
MARCH '45

By this time further reinforcements arrived with the 3rd Battalion and a fourth company was formed under the command of Barnay Du Boulay. On 1st March the Guards Battalions heard of their next task.

The Division was to drive through Goch to Kevelaer and then advanced past the village of Kapellen to the high ground around Bonninghardt on the main cross-roads south of Wesel. The Armoured Battalion joined the 3rd Battalion and started to move at half past one in the morning of the 4th March. The Irish Guards Group moved through Goch, Kevelaer and Winnekendonk. The roads were so bad that they had to leave all except track vehicles and jeeps behind in the rear of Kevelaer. From there on the men rode on the back of tanks.

The Irish Group attempted to proceed through the village of Hamb up to high ground. Light was failing but it was vital to push on through the village. There was now heavy shelling and mortaring in the village and the leading Coy-Sqn were held up at the forward edge of Hamb. A considerable number of casualties took place when the Coy following was moving up. By now it was pitch dark and further advance was out of the question. The 3rd Battalion consolidated their position with No.2 Coy in front and No.1 Coy out on the right flank whilst No.4 Coy watched over Bn HQ and the rear. Throughout the evening the shelling was both heavy and accurate. It was obvious that the Battalion needed to have a position on the high ground and No.2 Coy were ordered to push on and capture a small feature. Lieutenant Bobby O'Grady, supported by Lieutenant Whitfield-Edwards and his troop from the Second Battalion were ordered to seize this ground. Only nine men of the platoon and O'Grady managed to reach the objective with Whitfield-Edwards and two tanks. They were surrounded by Germans at very close quarters on all sides, but they had reached their objective and they held on to it.

* * *

Thursday 1st March 1945
Willie has gone off on the unpleasant job of unearthing the remains of the poor fellows who were killed in the last attack. It appears that a Brigade had to take the place at the finish and still it proved a tough nut to crack. Rain today which was a nuisance. Brian and I 'span the bar' with No3 pl. Then I fired up the radio. Things pretty easy now most of the guns seem to have moved further off. The sun came out later. Edward was found & John Kennedy.

Friday 2nd March
We got some horses and saddled them up. In the afternoon football was on the menu. All trucks to be loaded by tonight. We are to move at 1am. Everything is loaded up we are to go to Weeze & thence to Sepen. At 2100hrs message no move till 0930hrs. We had dinner and then went to bed. Sun and Snow.

Saturday 3rd March
All ready to move by 0930 hrs another message no move before 1100hrs still another message no more move before 1800hrs terrible rigmarole of pickup trucks. Americans apparently captured Geldem and are on the way to Issum. Now on one hours notice from 1800hrs. Good sun most of the day. I went for a ride this morning and got thrown rather infra dig.

To: Mrs P.H. Morrissey
           11 Wilberforce Road, Southsea Hants

No1 Coy
3rd Battalion Irish Guards
B.L.A
3rd March [1945]

My darling Baba and Pat,

I am afraid there is only time for a hurried note but I hope it gets there all the same. Did you receive my last one I wonder? We have been pretty busy lately as you have probably seen from the news. I think I can now tell you that poor Edward was killed a while back R.I.P. He was shot by a German machine gun and his loss to the Bn and especially No1 Coy is very, very great. He was the finest Coy Comdr one could wish for in action. Claude was wounded and did remarkably well. Only Willie and I remain now. We have now got Chris Dodd as Coy Comdr and Brian Russell is a Pl. Comdr in the same Coy. Someday I'll tell you all about it but I can't right now. The whole thing is terribly sad. The only consolation is that he died instantly.

Well, my darlings, the war news is extremely good I only pray to God that it won't be long before I can get back and see you all. The Americans are doing splendidly and so for that matter all the boys on the West. The going as you can imagine is not very exciting and though it's quite dry we are having small snow storms and the mud is still there. I believe the weather your way is pretty mild. I wrote to Cherub but as I don't know her address I have sent it via you will you forward it on please. I had rather fun today I got a horse and saddled her up or rather one of my platoon did and then I rode around on him. Actually it's a her and we call her 'Mary of Arnhem'. She threw me this morning and then gave me a hefty kick with one of her hind legs. I was most annoyed because in throwing me she broke a grand German baton which I had been carrying around and was keeping as a souvenir. No more for the present. Thanks for 200 players which fetched up OK. Tons and tons of love to you from your loving son Peter XXX

To: Captain P.H. Morrissey M.B.E.R.N.
        R N Barracks, Portsmouth Hants

No1 Coy
3rd Battalion Irish Guards
B.L.A
3rd March [1945]

Dear Captain,

I have not written to you for quite a while so I thought I'd send off a hurried line to let you know that there's not much news. That is not much that can be disclosed right here and now. But as you can see by the official stuff big news is abroad and great things look like happening. It would be too wonderful if all this hell would cease and we could return. If it's the Burma Liberating Army for me what chance of a staff job with Uncle Tony [Brigadier Tony Filose] I wonder. I think I have had just about enough of infantry slogging and all that goes with it. There one hopes that it won't take me but I'm afraid under 25 and not married are on the list so either I'll have to get married or else get a staff job or I suppose be a bloody fool and fight it out. On the face of things here at the moment the highest morale is held and optimism reigns supreme. I only hope to God the so and so's will give up right away. And so save some lives. It's a pretty bad state of affairs when you refused to give an address to an audience and pass the 'baby' onto some poor young officer. Think of the publicity you've thrown away. You have got your picture in the local rag anyhow!!

… Well skipper, as I said afore there is no news to write but I still keep that diary and after it's all over we can go over it together not that it's very interesting but still it will help me to remember. Keep yourself well and don't go to the cinema if Baba says you're not to. Loads and loads of love to you from Peter

PS I shall send one of these to Baba

Sunday 4th March

Moved off 0100hrs and travelled in TCVs all night via Goch (flattenened) Weeze (equally so) waited on road outside Kevelaer for about seven hours. Why the hell we had to miss a nights sleep just to wait on the road Lord only knows. The rain pelted down and we were all feeling pretty miserable. Had a meal and then got into the tanks. Travelled like this nearly as far as Reneple and waited there an hour. Bit of arty shooting then a plan was made for the Irish group to capture the village of Hamb. No.2 Coy 3 squadron leading No.1 Coy No.1 squad behind my last attack before Rhine was crossed.

Monday 5th March

Lt O'Grady, Lt Neil Whitfield Tank c/o, captured high ground
I left for snipers course in S-Hertogenbosch [19th March – 4th April]
rejoined 3rd Bn in Germany.

Belgium Jan 45 – I feel mighty tough – yes sir – mighty tough

To: Mrs P.H. Morrissey
        11 Wilberforce Road, Southsea Hants

No1 Coy
3rd Battalion Irish Guards
B.L.A
8th March [1945]

My Dearest Baba,

... You will have heard probably by now but we lost poor old Edward. I am not sure if I told you or not but he was killed some time back by a Spandau (machine gun). Awful bad luck he did magnificently and is a terrific loss to us all. Claude was wounded and has therefore gone back. I don't know if he is in England or not.

Willie Moore our other platoon commander has just been awarded the M.C. he did a damn fine piece of work a while ago. Is pretty good that and I'm frightfully glad. You know Baba it's awful to think of all the officers who have been with me since I joined the company and now I am only one left of the original lot. Brian Russell has joined the company and is in fine form poor old Brian I think it's rather shook him the change over from England to this. He has only just come out after nearly 2 years back home. He spent the last year at the 1st Bn in Scotland. He will be alright though once he gets acquainted with the form. The news as usual is terrific in the papers but as far as we are concerned in this place mortars and shells are still as real as ever. However we are in high hopes that by containing Jerry this end of the front the Americans will be able to push on and catch 'em all in the rear. Good to hear they are across the Rhine isn't it!? What we want to know is why can't we do the spectacular drives against little or no opposition and let the Yanks contain them. I see in the paper that even the places we (the Micks) capture are being allocated (by the journalists) to the glory of the Canadians too bad isn't it?! Still what the hell so long as someone does the job.

....Give my love to the captain and loads and loads of love to you from Peter XXX

To: Mrs P.H. Morrissey
        11 Wilberforce Road, Southsea Hants

No1 Coy
3rd Battalion Irish Guards
B.L.A
14th March [1945]

Baba Darling,

... My dear I was very fortunate indeed the other day. I had a wee piece of shrapnel come straight through the back of my steel helmet. It's a wonderful souvenir!! I am sure hanging onto it. It was only a very small piece but it went in and I think has come out now anyhow is nothing much but rather interesting. I'll bring the tin hat back and show you. Really proud of it. The horsey pastime has blown over and quite a bit has happened since then. I think I showed old Mary of Arnhem who was boss before we left!! I hope when this war is done I can get in some riding over the other side of the Rhine. There should be some pretty good horses roundabout.

I was sorry to hear Patricia has to prolong her stay at the cypher school. But perhaps it will be all for the best in the long run. At any rate it means she won't have to go overseas so soon. And though she wants to go badly I certainly don't want her to go before I get back. Lord knows when I shall get back on leave. I am due for it now but you know the army. There are still masses of people to go before me. Even now Baba there is only one other platoon commander who has been in the Battalion longer than I have. It hardly sounds credible but it's true. I put it down to all the prayers being said at home. There have been times when praying was the only answer.

Do you really think the Japs will cave in before this show is over here. It would be too marvellous but somehow I can't see it happening. They are more fanatical than the Jerry's and Lord knows they are hard enough fighters when cornered. Did you ever read Frenchman's Creek by Daphne Du Maurier. I rather enjoyed it and should love to see the film. There seems to be some very good shows on in London these days. By the way don't write coffee on the outside as if you do it will be cancelled or rather collared by the customs no foodstuffs are supposed to be sent out to foreign countries.

Must stop now to get this off I'll write again soon as possible.

Lots and lots of love to you both from Peter

Items collected in Europe

CHAPTER 9
APRIL / MAY '45

Having successfully completed a three-week sniper course in Shertogenbosch my father rejoined the 3rd Battalion in early April between Hamburg and Bremen.

The final weeks of the war gave the Micks no respite. On 1st April the Irish Guards Group drove through Haksbergen to Enschede. From here they continued on though Oldenzaal and then turned eastwards for Germany. It was shortly after this that Lieutenant Peter Cuffe of No. 2 Squadron, 2nd Battalion, and Brian Russell of the 3rd Battalion, were both killed in the town of Gildenhaus.

On the morning of the 12th the Irish Group crossed the Hase Canal into Loningen and then travelled eastwards up the road to Essen. On 21st April one of the final actions the Irish Guards were involved in during the war was at Wistedt where Guardsman E. Charlton was to be awarded a posthumous Victoria Cross following an eye witness statement from a German officer who took part in the attack that Charlton tried to prevent.

On 29th April the Irish Group advanced to Hasedorf and on 2nd May they halted at Estorf and Ohlendorf.

The war and the fighting petered out but not before one more officer from the 3rd Battalion was killed, Lieutenant Sebastian Hogg, on 2nd May, three days before unconditional surrender of all the German armed forces took place in North West Germany.

Finally, my Father got the leave he so desired and as irony would have it made his way back from London to rejoin his Battalion on 8th May 1945, V.E. Day.

* * *

To: Mrs P.H. Morrissey
        11 Wilberforce Road, Southsea Hants

No1 Coy
3rd Battalion Irish Guards
B.L.A
5th April [1945]

My dearest Baba and Pat,

.....Well, anyway, let's forget the war and tell one what you have been doing. I am afraid I am way behind my mail and so I have quite a lot of letters to thank you for. I sure do envy you back there being able to drive around like Royalty. I guess it should take me for a spot of leave pretty soon. Before I come though I must get a license and have a shot at driving on the left hand side of the road instead of the right. When I first took a motorcycle out here I forgot completely about different sides of the road and very nearly ended up under a troop carrier coming the other way. Dopey thing!

I hear Brighton is just a mass of humanity it must be perfectly marvellous!! I have met a very good fellow called Jack Hunter in the Queen's Own Camerons of Canada he is in the same outfit as Hughie and was stationed near Brighton for some time. He is a great fellow and comes from Toronto. When we get back to Blighty I am asking him to stay a while if that's okay by you!

... Must close now keep smiling and God bless you both. Tons and tons of love from Peter XXX

To: Mrs P.H. Morrissey
        11 Wilberforce Road, Southsea Hants

No1 Coy
3rd Battalion Irish Guards
B.L.A
16th April [1945]

My darling ones,

.....Baba isn't it awfully sad about poor Brian R.I.P. I liked him awfully, and he was killed while I was away. Shot by a sniper. He was such a nice kid too. It seems such a pity that anyone has to get killed at this stage of the war. And Peter Cuffe also was killed R.I.P. He was another friend of mine in the 2nd Bn. Well I suppose that is war but it seems so terrible.

.....You ask me very seriously what I would like for my 21st well honestly I don't know what I want, I can't say that I want very much. I should very much like to have a signet ring with the good old elephant on it. But I guess it's better to leave that sort of thing until the war is over and one can get things. I guess the best present of the lot would be a spot of leave from the Army what say you?

Goodnight darlings and look after yourself I should be seeing you soon I hope. Must close now. I'll be writing again as soon as possible, lots and lots of love to you both Peter.

To: Mrs P.H. Morrissey
        11 Wilberforce Road, Southsea Hants

No1 Coy
3rd Battalion Irish Guards
B.L.A
Germany
Thursday April [1945]

My darling Baba and Pat,

I'm just seizing a moment of spare time to scribble a line to you. Things are certainly much brighter on the bigger picture but it is absolutely maddening to read that the war is over when unfortunately only too many boys are getting killed all the time. It's certainly too ridiculous.

I am temporarily attached to number 2nd Coy at the moment but if you just address my letters 3rd Bn I will get the mail all right. Great thunderstorm yesterday after one of the hottest days I have known this year. It was stifling. By the way I think I told you the coffee turned up and was great could you send some more or is it hard to get.

… Anyhow as soon as I know the date or approx. date I shall let you know. Perhaps beginning of May or sooner maybe.

I told you about poor old Brian and Peter Cuffe; they were both killed some time ago and it is very sad. I do hope it will all be over soon. I cannot see how it can possibly last very much longer but these damned Jerries are devils for sticking out under the most absurd conditions.

I am thinking of you all and praying hard for peace and the day when we shall meet again. Thank you for your prayers and candles. I managed to get to mass on Sunday and I was so pleased. I prayed for you all. Patricia and Cherub will be on leave now I expect hope you are all having a wonderful time. I saw a few pictures of the sea coast open to bathers. Have you been swimming yet. What about the 2,000 Guineas any bets these days. I haven't played cards since I won all the cash. But I expect I shall when I get short again. I sent a £15 cheque off to the bank the other day which should come in useful. Are there any good shows in London these days? Did I tell you I saw Henry V film whilst I was away from the Battalion I enjoyed it rather but I thought it very much overrated, have you seen it I wonder.

Well must stop now. Keep well and cheerful I am simply longing to see you all again. Please God it won't be too long.

Lots and lots of love to you both from your loving son Peter XXX

To: Mrs P.H. Morrissey
        11 Wilberforce Road, Southsea Hants

No1 Coy
3rd Battalion Irish Guards
B.L.A
8th May [1945]

My dearest darling Baba,

Thank you so much for the lovely leave I was able to spend. I do hope you are not too tired after it. As I'm afraid I must have made an awful lot of extra work for you. But I did so enjoy it. I am going to write to D. and enclose it in this letter. I expect he will be much better for going into hospital even if it is going to take longer. It was a pity but of course quite unavoidable and next time we shall have to make up for it.

Well, darling, I haven't come very far yet. But as this will be my last chance of writing this side I am taking it. After the train had passed Havant, two girls, who were in the same compartment as myself, suddenly asked me if it was the train to Chichester and as it was a fast train they had to wait till we reached Hazelmere before being able to get out. And they were all spruced up in their "glad rags" obviously going to a party. They never realised it was a Sunday service!!

When we arrived in London I had the one helluva journey by underground to Victoria. I thought I could change at Piccadilly but it should have been Charing X. The tube was packed you could hardly breathe. Anyway I struggled along and managed to make Victoria by 9:30. I dumped my baggage in the Grosvenor and with my tongue hanging out made a bee-line for the American Bar. Do you think I could get a drink? I hadn't a hope everywhere was sold out I wandered around outside and the same thing greeted me sold out! It was awful! I was so dry too. However I went to the smoking room of the Grosvenor and waited and finally at 10:30 I managed to get a gin and ginger ale for 5/- but I tried hard to phone only there was such a crowd. And I had no small change and the girl who usually operates the phones had gone celebrating. The crowds in the streets were enormous. All singing and shouting and waving flags.

Then at 11 I went to the barrier and we waited till nearly 12 before they let us in. However after we got in I did get a corner seat and there was a Naafi Cafe so I was able to get a cup of coffee and a ham sandwich and cake.

There were some very amusing incidents on the station which helped the time to go. One Capt was so tight he could hardly stand and another very merry soldier came along and made some rather amusing remarks. I met the fellow I had travelled over with and we got a seat together. The train pulled out about 12. And we arrived in Folkestone about 2. They took us to a rather nice hotel for the night and you could buy drinks and then I went to bed about 3. Got up about 9 and have just had breakfast. I expect we will sail this morning around about 12.

...

Lots and lots of love to you darling and once again thanks for the heavenly leave.

Goodbye and God bless Peter

As ADC to the Supreme Commander and Military Governor
of the Anglo-American Zone, Trieste

CHAPTER 10
POST-WAR SERVICE

My father re-joined the Battalion on 10th May 1945. In his diary he makes mention of a concentration camp at Sandbostel. This camp was relieved on 29th April by the Grenadiers, accompanied by some Irish Guards. I suspect my father was on leave at this time, but he may have gone to the camp shortly after he returned to Germany. Descriptions paint the camp as being as bad as those photographed and publicised from Belson and Buchenwald; there is plenty of information on line regarding Sandbostel.

On 19th May the Battalion was given orders to move to the South and by 21st May they were spread out over a large area South West of Bremen. Their responsibilities were to include immediate control of the civilian population; the collection of all arms and ammunition in the area; and the arrest and imprisonment of any self-demobilised members of the Wehrmacht.

On 28th May the Battalion moved into the area of Westertinke in order to take over control of an Internment camp. They remained there until mid-June, when they found themselves in the area of Rosrath-Noffnungsthal in command of a camp at Wahnerheide containing 10,000 Russian Displaced Persons.

My father was finally posted home to the 1st Battalion Irish Guards on 28th July 1945, just short of a year since the day he arrived in France.

On 14th January 1946 he attended an officers' accounts course at the Guards Depot prior to being posted to the Training Battalion on 8th April 1946. However this proved not to be very helpful as he got in a spot of bother as The President of the Mess Committee, PMC, and was charged with negligence – although I rather suspect he was just out of his depth, "he allowed the Mess Accounts to become hopelessly entangled". Perhaps the irony is that in his civilian life he worked in the City of London for over 30 years! The presiding officer was none other than his previous Commanding Officer, Joe Vandeleur, who by now was the Regimental Lieutenant Colonel. The matter was dropped and shortly after on 24th July 1946 he was posted to Italy as ADC to Lieutenant General Sir Terence Airey, who was appointed Supreme Commander and Military Governor of the Anglo-American Zone in Trieste.

There is no account of that period other than anecdotal stories of being pulled over by the American Military Police for driving a three-star general's car late at night, or participating in numerous poker games conveniently attended by the Commanding Officer of the US Military Police!

As can be seen by the photographs of Trieste of that time (overleaf), there can be little doubt that this was a respite following the events that had taken place in North West Europe and in advance of him leaving the Army on 23rd April 1947 before joining civilian life.

Like so many of my father's generation, he volunteered to fight for King and Country, and like so many when asked, "What did you do in the war?", "Not a great deal" would be the answer… and the conversation would change to something else. A religious family man, it was appropriate that he should join the Micks. Often the envy of the British Army, the Micks are a family regiment adored by all who have served in it – from the humble guardsman to Field Marshall Earl Alexander of Tunis, His Royal Highness

Prince John of Luxembourg and of course to Her Majesty Queen Elizabeth The Queen Mother, who for so many years gave up much of her time to be with us… to name but a few.

GEORGETTE

Peter, Venice, St Marks Square, 1946

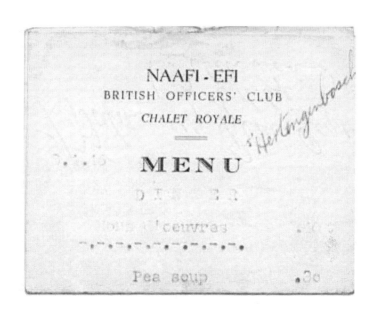

NAAFI - EFI
BRITISH OFFICERS' CLUB
CHALET ROYALE
—
MENU

Pea soup

Belgium, Holland and Germany
2nd Bn, Irish Guards
KILLED OR DIED OF WOUNDS

Number	Rank	Name
324096	Lieutenant	P.A. Cuffe.
139211	Captain	H.C.H. Fitzherbert.
268994	Lieutenant	W.C.T. McFetridge.
240008	Lieutenant	J.C. O'Brien.
132247	Major	D.A. Peel, M.C.
268994	Lieutenant	J.A.P. Swann.

3rd Bn. Irish Guards
KILLED OR DIED OF WOUNDS

172774	Captain	W.R.R.S. Bruce.
93020	Major	M.V. Dudley.
106178	Major	G.E. Fisher-Rowe.
330864	Lieutenant	A. Geraghty.
260227	Lieutenant	W.H.J. Hogg.
253922	Lieutenant	H.O.C. Kennard.
94576	Major	D.M. Kennedy, M.C.
307921	Lieutenant	R.P. O'Kelly.
219069	Captain	E.E. Rawlence (M.I.D.)
278612	Lieutenant	B.B. Russell.
228328	Lieutenant	P.G.E. Sarsfield-Hall

LIEUTENANT H. MICHAEL A. CAMBIER

Unit: Anti-Tank Platoon, Support Company,
               156th Parachute Battalion
Army No.:   226876

The following story, *The Murder of Lieutenant H. M. A. Cambier*, was written and researched by Philip Reinders of the Arnhem Battle Research Group.

This is the story of Lieutenant Michael Cambier at Arnhem where he commanded the Anti Tank platoon of the 156 The Parachute Regiment. For some of the details I am indebted to his friend Ronnie Adams who commanded the Mortar platoon in the same Battalion as well as to some former members of the Dutch Resistance.

Michael was born into an Army family in Batavia on 9th September 1921. He was the only child of Colonel and Mrs Valentine Cambier, his father being a regular soldier in the Indian Army. He was educated in England at Welbury Park Preparatory School and at Ampleforth College from where he gained an Open Exhibition to New College Oxford. He was up at Oxford in 1940 and took a shortened Degree Course in mathematics before being commissioned into the Royal Artillery.

He was posted abroad and reached Egypt in time to take part in the Battle of El Alamein. Shortly after, he volunteered for parachuting, did his training at the Middle East

Parachute School and was posted to 156 Battalion which was then stationed at Jenin in Palestine in early 1943. He first commanded a platoon in B Company and was with them Tunisia and subsequently in Italy, when 4th Parachute Brigade took part in the sea landing at Taranto, in the subsequent fighting Michael was Mentioned in Despatches. On the Battalions return to England in December 1943 he took over command of the recently formed Anti Tank platoon in Support Company.

On 18th September 1944, the second day of the Arnhem Operation, he was dropped with the rest of the 4th Parachute Brigade on Ginkel Heath. The next 24 hours the Battalion suffered very heavy losses in its attempt to reach Arnhem. It was during this action that Michael was slightly wounded in the foot on 19th September.

He refused to be evacuated and stayed with his platoon. The last that Ronnie Adams saw of him, he was busily engaged in attempting to withdraw his 6 pounder Anti Tank guns towards Oosterbeek which was South of the main railway line to Arnhem. Such a move was difficult because the only culvert under the railway embankment was partially obstructed by a supply container with a chute which had "roman candled" and come into the culvert with part of its roof. The railway was being swept by enemy fire and the only alternative route open to Michael and his guns was to retrace his steps along the embankment to Wolfheze where there was a level crossing. It would seem that like many others he did not get to Wolfheze and the next that we know of his progress is that he was taken with other wounded prisoners to the St Joseph Hospital in Apeldoorn some miles north of Arnhem.

On 25th September he was put on a Hospital train bound for the Neurenberg Hospital camp, on this train he joined up with Lieutenant Raymond Bussell of A Company of the 3rd Parachute Battalion who had been wounded in the arm and they decided to try to escape. They made a hole in the carriage floor through which they dropped down when the opportunity presented itself. They made their escape when the train was approximately 10 miles from a village called Bathmen, just to the East of the Dutch town of Deventer which is situated on the river IJssel.

It was then the afternoon of the 26th September, they walked until they came to a farm. The woman who lived there was in the employ of a Mr Jansen and she took them to his large house in Bathmen which was called "The Menop". They were to stay in his house for 7 days during which they were given civilian clothes and had their wounds attended to by a local doctor. On the evening of 1st October, which was a Sunday, they were put in the care of a student from Amsterdam who was a member of the local resistance. He told Mr Jansen that he would take them as far as the river IJssel which was only about 7 miles from Bathmen, he hoped they would be able to cross the river and eventually reach the Allied lines. To do so, however they would still have had to cross the Neder Rijn and the Waal (much more formidable obstacles than the IJssel). They were, of course now wearing civilian clothes having left their uniforms behind at "the Menop". They were not without Dutch money because Raymond Bussell had managed to exchange some of the money which had been issued to officers for use in the occupied territories for some Dutch guilders. They were first taken by their guide to a small place called T'Joppe which was near to Gorssel which was only a few miles from Bathmen but which was close by the IJssel.

They did not stop there however but were taken to another farm called "Braamkolk" in a small place called

Eefde which was further to the South and nearer to Zutphen, this belonged to the same family as T'Joppe and was regarded as being safer. They reached there on 2nd October having passed some German soldiers on the way and it is probable that they spent the night there. On leaving the farm, they were challenged by a German soldier who asked them for their papers. German soldiers were very much in evidence in this area because they were busy building a defensive line to the East of the IJssel. The son of the farmer, who was very young at the time, says he can remember seeing three strangers walking round a shed. They were asked to produce their papers which only the Dutch guide could do. Michael and Raymond had been told to say "verloren" which is Dutch for "lost", if they were ever challenged and asked for their papers. The German had no idea that he was faced with 2 British Officers but he ordered them all into his vehicle and took them to the police station at Zutphen. Later they were transferred to the police station at Gorssel where a Dutch policeman released the student from the Resistance because he could find nothing wrong with his papers and in any event he was sympathetic to the cause.

Michael and Raymond had no reason at this stage to believe that they would be treated other than as Prisoners of War. Had they done so they might have contemplated another break, but clearly they had no idea of the immediate danger they were in. Unfortunately, whilst they were still in the police station a Dutch member of the SD (Sicherheidsdienst), the German Security Police, came into the station and when he discovered that the 2 men in civilian clothes were British officers he informed his superior who was Untersturmfuhrer Ludwig Heinneman. When Heinneman heard that the Dutch policeman had allowed the Dutch civilian to go free he was immediately arrested and sent to a Concentration Camp from which he returned after the War although by then he was a broken man.

On 10th October Michael and Raymond were taken to the local SD Headquarters, this was Villa "T'Selsham" at Vorden a town a few miles to the South-East of Zutphen. Here they were duly interrogated by 2 members of the SD, one of whom spoke English. Both Michael and Raymond refused to give any other information than their name, rank and number. After their interrogation, they were taken downstairs and confronted by Heinneman who accused them of being spies and terrorists, their hands were tied behind their backs and they were told that they would be shot. They were taken outside and shot in the head by Heinneman himself using a captured Sten gun. The executions took place early in the afternoon of the 10th October and they were buried in the lawn at the front of the Villa together with three Jehovah's witnesses who were executed by Heinneman the same day, the lawn was then set on fire to remove any trace.

On 9th June 1945, members of the War Crimes Commission, a former member of the Dutch Resistance and some local civilians exhumed the bodies of the 2 Officers and the Jehovah's witnesses. Raymond Bussell still had the money he had exchanged with Mr Jansen, 57 Guilders.

Before he left Michael had written a letter to his mother, which he had requested should be given to the first British Officer Mr Jansen met. Not aware of Michael's fate he wrote to Mrs Cambier after the war to enquire what happened to him and heard from her the terrible news.

Ludwig Heinneman was arrested on 18th March 1946, after a trial he was executed by a firing squad at Arnhem on

10th February 1947. He was found guilty of many War Crimes including the murder of some 70 people. He had nothing to say for himself except that he did what his superiors had told him to do - "Befehl ist Befehl" (orders are orders). Other members of the SD who were present at Vorden were also arrested and spent some time in prison but they were not long.

It has taken me 4 years to find out what happened at Vorden on that fateful day in October 1944, but I do not begrudge the time or money spent. Whenever I am around Vorden I make a point of laying flowers on Michael and Raymond's graves which are in the General Cemetery there, as though by some people they will never be forgotten there is nobody to remember them when September comes round.

Philip Reinders, 1999

GLOSSARY

11 armoured	11th Armoured Division
1st Grens	Grenadier Guards
2 I/C [or 2nd i/c]	Second in Command
7 Divs	7th Armoured Division
A/P	Anti Personnel
a/Tk	Anti Tank
Arromanches	Mulberry artificial harbour, D-day landing beaches
Arty	Artillery
B.L.F.	British Liberation Force
B.O.A.	British Overseas Airways Corporation (BOAC) was the British state-owned airline created in 1939 by the merger of Imperial Airways and British Airways Ltd. It continued operating overseas services throughout World War II.
Bn	Battalion
Bn HQ	Battalion Headquarters
Box mines	The Schu-mine 42 (Shoe-mine), also known as the Schützenmine 42, was a German anti-personnel mine used during the WW2.
C.O.	Commanding Officer
Colys	Coldstream Guards
Comd	Commander
Comdr	Commander
Coy	Company
C.W.L.	Catholic Women's League
C.W.T.	Hundredweight
D.C.L.I.	Duke of Cornwall's Light Infantry
Divs [or Div]	Division
F.O.O.	Forward Operating Officer

Frs	Francs
GAD	Guards Armoured Division
Gds	Guards
Gdsm	Guardsman
Huns	Germans
I	Infantry
I.G. Group	Irish Guards Group
i/c	In Command
Jerry	German
L/Cpl	Lance Corporal
L.M.G.	Light Machine Gun
M.C.	Military Cross
ME109	The Messerschmitt Bf 109 was a German World War II fighter aircraft that was the backbone of the Luftwaffe's fighter force.
N.C.O.	Non-commissioned officer
Naafi	Navy army and air force institute
O.C.T.U.	Officer Cadet Training Unit
P.O.W.	Prisoner of war
P.T.	Physical Training
Pl	Platoon
Pl Comds	Platoon Commanders
PMC	President Mess Committee
R.H.U.	Reinforcement Holding Unit
recce	reconnaissance
S.G.	Scotts Guards
Spandaus [or Sp]	The Maschinengewehr 08, or MG 08, was the German Army's standard machine gun in World.
Spits	Spitfires
STpt	Start Point
T.C.V.	Troop Carrying Vehicle
Teller mines	The Teller mine was a German-made antitank mine common in World War II.
TFO	(till further orders)
T.G.	Thank God !
Tr Bn	Training Battalion
W.	Weapons
W.G.	Welsh Guards

The Irish Guards Commemorative Tour
9th – 13th September 1994

Seated from Left to Right:
Major Tinker Taylor M.C., Colonel William Harvey Kelly M.B.E.,
Captain Rupert Mahaffy, Captain Peter Morrissey,
Lieutenant Brian Wilson C.B.E.